FLIPPING OUT OVER PROBATES

How to Find and Flip Your First Probate Property Without Cash, Credit, or Experience

Jason Lucchesi

Flipping Out Over Probates:

How to Find and Flip Your First Probate Property Without Cash, Credit, or Experience

ISBN: 978-0-578-63003-8

Cover design by Sooraj Mathew

Edited by Hilary Jastram

FLIPPING OUT OVER PROBATES

TABLE OF CONTENTS

RESOURCES

1. Free training from Jason Lucchesi — www.youtube.com/jasonlucchesi

    Make sure to become a YouTube channel subscriber today and receive instant notifications when new uploads have been completed.

2. Check out the best Real Estate Investing podcast on the planet:

    The No Flipping Excuses Show – www.BestDamnInvestingPodcast.com

3. A top software for putting together deal evaluations and private money presentations. Try out the free trial of the software today.

    www.RehabValuator.com

4. If you need a reliable CRM to help automate and streamline your real estate investing business, then look no further. Check them out and give it a test drive!

    www.FreedomSoft.com

5. If you want to reach a ton of people without spending hours on the phone, then you need this ringless voicemail system in your business.

    www.SlyBroadcast.com

6. Don't spend hours and hours doing your own direct mail. You can use these folks to do it all for you and

see some of the best responses from marketing that works.

www.YellowLettersComplete.com

7. If you're having a tough time managing your leads and tracking key performance indicators, then this is the software you need in your business. You need to be tracking the metrics in your business, and this makes everything simple.

   www.InvestorFuse.com

8. If you need funding for your rehabs and rentals, this is the place to go. They have several lenders bidding to do business with you. You can get responses quickly, so you don't ever lose out on closing a deal.

   www.CiX.com

9. If you need a reliable virtual assistant to assign tasks to, then look no further. Find several VAs to hire for your business in a matter of 1-2 days. We've been personally using them for years, and I highly recommend them.

   www.UpWork.com

10. If you're looking for one of the most reliable dialer systems, you've found it in Mojo. Our entire team uses it, including our virtual assistants. It's so easy to upload a list and start calling people immediately that you can easily knock out thousands of calls weekly.

    www.MojoSells.com

11. Don't spend a ton of money on a fancy web designer. Save your money and invest in a Carrot website. You can get ranked in the top searches of Google easily while having a solid flow of leads dripping into investing business. All the smart investors use this service because it simply works!
    www.Carrot.com

12. This is a free skip tracing service. The accuracy of finding data is amazing. We use the service when we need to find contact information for homeowners.
    www.FastPeopleSearch.com

APPRECIATION & PROCEEDS

A huge Thanks to my kids Brady, Gavin, and Cordelia. You guys are a huge part of what I do. You guys can do anything you set your minds to! Never give up and always follow your dreams!

Much love and appreciation to my Mom and Dad!

*****

100% of the profits generated from *Flipping Out Over Probate* book sales are being donated to the following 501(c)(3) nonprofit organizations:

Beat Kid's Cancer
Mission statement:
Beat Kid's Cancer is a nonprofit that assists local families battling childhood cancer with living expenses and helps provide Christmas gifts for the families each year. Their goal is to eventually fund a research grant to help end this disease.
www.BeatKidsCancerTexas.com

Veteran's Best Friend Indiana

Mission statement:

Professional dog trainers partner veterans with rescue dogs in Indiana as pets, at no cost to the veteran. A dog can help ease anxiety, loneliness, depression, even PTSD symptoms. Pet ownership encourages love and acceptance, companionship, responsibility, interaction, and exercise. www.VeteransBestFriendIN.com

INTRODUCTION

You're about to discover one of the most profitable and rewarding deal-flipping strategies on the planet. One of the hottest strategies hardly anyone uses.

Most people aren't like you. The average person wants the reward of something which is freakishly easy to do delivered to them on a silver frickin' platter. In this book, you'll be given an opportunity, unlike anything you've witnessed before, which will give you an unfair advantage in your marketplace. It'll be simple to execute, and you can see results lightning-fast, yet you'll have to be willing to put in the hard work and commitment. It's not going to be easy, but I know you can do it.

Make a promise to yourself right here, and now that you'll live each day moving forward like you're preparing to play in the biggest football game of the year. You're the quarterback, and your teammates are depending on you.

It's time for you to win the game using strategies for finding properties and getting them under contract, so they will allow you to make big money with whatever exit strategy you choose. Whether that be wholesale—meaning you want to fix and flip it—or you want to keep the property for your own income-producing portfolio, the choice is yours to make, and it can pay off in different ways.

Several methods exist for you to find properties and secure them at discounts. When you use what I'm about to share with you, you can make smart real estate investing decisions. One of the best ways I've found to find deals is through individuals who are going through a difficult time.

This doesn't mean you are setting out to take advantage of people who are going through a hardship. What I mean is that sometimes people find themselves in situations where they are losing their houses, for one reason or another, and they need help. What you will learn in this book will allow you to help them.

Maybe you've gone through some hardships yourself. I've been through hardships just like anyone else, and as a result, I've always wanted to figure out how to find and help people who have just lost a loved one.

I remember when my grandfather passed away. The house was in my grandmother's name, and once she started failing and died, then my mom, aunt, and uncle were the ones who took over the property as the heirs. My aunt was the executor of the estate, and it was difficult to liquidate the property. My aunt lives in Wisconsin. My uncle was going to move closer to her. And my mom lived about an hour away from the property. Their plan was for the property to sit vacant because nobody wanted to assume responsibility for it. When dealing with individuals who have just lost a loved one, I have learned they typically don't want to move into the property. They want to gather all the items and then distribute them amongst family, especially if everybody is on good terms with each other. And yes, there are instances where family members do not get along.

When my grandmother passed, it was a very difficult time. One of the things I wanted to find out when I became a real estate investor back in 2008 was, *how can I find these families and offer them my help, so they won't have to worry about the property*?

This type of lead is called a probate. And that's what this entire book is about: finding people who have just lost a loved one and helping them through such an incredibly delicate time. After a loved one dies, the people left holding the property are vulnerable. It's difficult communicating with them and letting them know that you are there to help them.

When my family was trying to get through the loss of my grandfather, no one contacted my mom, nor my aunt or uncle, to see if they wanted to sell the property. No updates had been made to the property at all. Fortunately, the home was in a very good area where if the right investors saw it as an opportunity, they could make a substantial amount of money because it *was* massively outdated. That's a factor we're finding with probates. A lot of these properties are extremely outdated. Properties are dated back to the 70s, 60s and even the 50s. This presents a huge opportunity.

Two major issues that arise when a loved one passes are 1) suddenly, taxes are due, and 2) maintenance of the property has to be addressed. It's important that you stay on top of these tasks, so you won't have to worry about the city slapping the property with a code violation, deferred maintenance fees (applicable when you are rehabbing the property), property insurance, and utilities, etc. Also, the deceased may have collected a lot of items that the heirs or executor want, which could lead them to cleaning out the house and renting a dumpster that the majority of people don't have the time or money for. I view these circumstances as problems for the heirs and the executor of the estate. But we, as the real estate investors, can come in and solve many, if not all, of these problems.

Another problem that crops up is if the property is vacant, the heirs don't want to bother with having the property secured, and so it might not be protected from vandalism or other threats. If the person in charge of the estate lives near the subject property, they might not want the property to be managed by a property manager. Not to mention that most people do not want to have tenants because tenants equal problems, especially if the heirs live out-of-state. There are several things you can do to resolve these issues, of course. And these solutions are pretty obvious, still, what I've found over the years is that probates are a special circumstance. They offer a unique chance to get into a property because, as a lead source, they are almost untapped. The sensitivity of the circumstances makes most investors a little gun shy. In the case of securing property and flipping it, as I have written about in my prior books, *Right Flipping Now* and *Find the Flipping Deals,* most investors try to communicate once or twice, at a maximum, with the heirs or the executor of the estate. But then the attempt at communication stops. Most investors don't follow up after their second communication, that receives no response.

This book is designed to show you all of the intricacies of working with probates. It also explains what it really takes to create a successful and thriving business utilizing probates as one of your lead sources. It's up to you to decide if probates are going to be your main and only lead source. We use probates in addition to two other strategies in our business. But probates have always proved to be one of the best ways to contract a property at a great price and then flip it. We primarily wholesale properties, which means we don't keep them, and we also don't fix and flip them. Our goal is to find them, contract them, and then quickly wholesale them off for a profit. Since we've been doing business this way dating back to 2008, a lot of different strategies have affected this industry. In relation to the three strategies that we use, probates always outperform the others: bank-owned, tax deeds, expired listings, blogging, search engine optimization, pay-per-click ads, short sales, divorces, bankruptcy, low equity, subject-to, and listed properties.

As we review what you need to know, I hope to teach you that as long as you work this business, have the proper follow-up and communicate well with people; you're going to have a great opportunity to utilize probate within your business.

Many people get discouraged after sending off a direct mailer one time without receiving a response. When they don't get anything back, they throw in the towel. You have to realize this isn't a real estate business. It's a marketing business. If you are not marketing, you're not going to get the deals.

Don't worry about feeling like you need to know it all. Within this book, we'll talk about several different ways to execute your marketing. Whether you want to throw a small budget at your marketing, or rely on organic strategies, what I am about to teach you works.

When I first got started in the business, I had little money to my name. I had to figure out all the ways to make it work.

I want to save you some of the pain I've been through. That's why I've made this book very detailed. In writing this book, I've left no stone unturned. I used the knowledge I have gained, and that of my partners, to make sure you, as the reader, will have all the tools you need to make probate investing an investment tactic that allows you to thrive.

The worst thing that can happen to somebody is losing a loved one. They need people in their lives who can help them, who can save them worry. On top of losing the person they loved, now they've got this property they more than likely do not want. I would say nine out of every 10 individuals you meet will not want the property. Most of the time, they don't even want the items inside the house. Dealing with the house, and the possessions prolongs the pain of the people left behind. They want the probate process to be over as soon as possible. They also want to know, in the midst of their pain, they are being treated well. When all is said, they don't want anything to worry about.

You'll find as you get into buying probate properties, the heirs will sift through the items left behind, and maybe they'll find a few items they want. But for the most part, they'll sell the whole property to you as-is. They will see you as the problem solver.

There are two things I want you to keep in mind as you continue reading:

1. You are a marketer.
2. You are a problem solver.

This is a different mindset than most people have who work in this business. They will tell you: "I'm a real estate investor." When I hear those words come out of their mouths, I think *that's awesome. If you're a real estate investor and closing zero deals, then what kind of business do you really have*?

I think you can anticipate how I would answer that question. And I want better for you.

So, I'm going to explain to you the marketing. I'm going to explain to you the nuances you can use to become a problem-solver rather than some 1970s salesman on an infomercial trying to sell hand towels.

We're focusing on probates in this book so you can have a thriving business and one which will help people. That's what life is all about.

When it comes to probates, other real estate investors have been going about managing them in the wrong way. They haven't been taking care of the people left behind. They also haven't been helping them through a truly confusing and depressing time.

If you have the right mindset for diving into probates and utilizing everything at your disposal, as explained in this book, you can be 100% successful. All you have to do is simply follow this step-by-step format.

Everything I am sharing with you in this book, we teach to our high-end mastermind members. The only thing you're not receiving is me actually sitting next to you as you learn my process, and that's it.

If you want your business's probate strategy to thrive and give you the results you desire, you have to have the mindset for it. You're going to hear people say no to you. You need to accept what you have to do to put in the work. This business is simple: it requires hard work to see the results you desire. If probates were a snap, then every single person would be working this business. So go ahead, make it happen. I know you can do this.

I'm so excited you decided to pick up this book and that you are making the commitment to make probates work for you and the heirs left behind. Let's get to work! I will see you in the next chapter.

CHAPTER ONE: LAYING THE FOUNDATION

Before we take a deep dive into probates, It's important to lay down the foundation. We need to know exactly what probate is and how to go about processing a probate deal.

To get started, we can't just get probate leads from the recorder's office by firing off an email and waiting for them to respond. Trust me, we will get to that point where we will talk about utilizing this strategy, but right now, we want to discuss the multiple methods that you can profit from.

If you want to be the individual in your marketplace who is going to get the best leads—and you're reading this book (so you obviously want a strategy) to work in probates—I will always recommend and encourage you to have at least two or three different strategies in play. You don't want to count on one thing to bring in the business. Probates are one part of the foundation you are building in your company. Now, let's dig into what you need to know to stand out in the market so that you won't be viewed like every other investor.

When you start out, count on working hard. But also count on striking out and not getting any deals. It happens. In these methods we are covering in this book, you'll be able to start building your empire, and you'll know exactly which leads are going to be the best fit for you. This means you won't waste time.

This is a huge benefit to you already! But you will still need to get your feet wet, so remember, that, too, is a part of building your process.

Now, let's talk about what probate is.

When somebody dies, and their assets are distributed, these assets include both commercial and residential real estate. A lot of people have a common misunderstanding that if the deceased person had a will, they could avoid the probate process. That's not true. All real estate must go through the probate process unless a living trust has been set.

In later chapters, we'll discuss how you can find out who has a living trust, which is a huge strategy in itself. After working in this space for 10 years, I can say with confidence 99% of individuals who are going after probate are not going after those who have a trust set up. So, if you have questions concerning trusts, rest assured this topic will be covered in a later portion of this book. And yes, it's important to know this information, but it's also critical to know all the information pertaining to your deals as that influences how every aspect of the process works.

Defining Probate

Lexico defines probate as "The official proving of a will.[1]" In laymen's terms, probate proves the will is valid. Probate also pays debts and taxes left by the deceased. It distributes the remaining property according to the will. If there is no will, the court will appoint an estate representative. When this happens, it's difficult to get to the actual heir or executor of the estate since there wasn't really one set up.

In this case, you have to wait for either the representative of the estate or possibly a judge to appoint an individual to be in charge of the estate. Even when the judge appoints a person, you might run into a daughter, son, or another relative contesting the judge's ruling and wanting to be the executor of the estate.

Let's say an older individual passed, who didn't know how to set everything up properly before their death. There's no will, and there's no executor. When there is no will, the state appoints the executor who is called intestate. Meaning when a person dies without having a valid will in place, his or her property passes by what is called "intestate succession" to heirs according to state law. In other words, if you don't have a will, the state will make one for you. All 50 states have laws (or "statutes") of this kind on the books. If the deceased had children, one of those individuals could contest the appointment. They would come forward to the judge and ask to be granted executor of the estate. Most times, this will be granted. If it doesn't get granted, it usually means the judge would like additional information from whoever wants to be the executor.

Regardless of who is appointed, you can still get these properties at huge discounts. We're talking pennies on the dollar. Not many investors know how to acquire and implement probates in their business, though.

Not many people know how to implement the strategies we're going over in this book, either.

When we first started looking for probates in 2008, we would go to the county's assessor's office, and there was no line. No one else was there looking for probates. I religiously went to the assessor's office every week. My idea was to contact the people in charge of the probates as they were getting entered into the system at the assessor's office. I wanted to be one of the first individuals to acquire the probate paperwork to gather the information I needed to reach out to the heirs and talk about working together. I was excited to both help these people who needed an advisor in a trying moment of their life, and because I knew, probates require very little overhead. A one-person team can handle them.

If you're an individual who doesn't have a team completely set up yet, that's completely fine. Or maybe you already have a team in place. This book will be a great resource each of your team members should read. If you're that team member, hello! It's wonderful to meet you! I'm excited to help you learn probates. If you need additional help, please refer to the resources page at the beginning of this book to get in touch with my team and me.

Probates fall into the category of having a low barrier to entry. Marketing costs will be minimal because depending on the county you're living in, or if you want to work with multiple counties, you're not going to send out thousands of mail pieces every month. Most likely, you'll send out only hundreds of direct mail pieces.

Our direct mail pieces do extremely well. We use a letter and postcard which are provided in this book. I'm giving it to you so you can get to work right away. Use it as-is (yes, please plagiarize it!) so you can start seeing results. Remember, this is just one option you can use to diversify your real estate investing strategies.

Adding probates to your business plan allows you to bring in an extra (at a bare minimum) one to two deals per month. How you will acquire these probate deals allows you to purchase the properties before they are even listed. These are great off-market properties your cash buyers will absolutely love. They will pay top dollar for them within about a week or two from you getting them under contract. Understand, I am not diving too deeply into the specifics here. Just know you are simply assigning the property—which I will explain in greater detail in a later chapter of this book.

We'll be talking about the contract you will use and the different types of strategies to apply to make sure you get top dollar for your properties.

Now, let's discuss how a probate property comes to be and the ins and outs of the deal.

What Happens When a Probate Case is Created?

The probate case is filed when somebody passes away. If there is a will, it is entered into the probate file. Then the court appoints the estate representative for the case if the will has one named. If the will does not name any one person as the executor, the court will appoint somebody, as I mentioned.

The executor or the state representative will assess all the assets and debts left behind from the deceased individual. The executor or state representative will get an appraisal of all the assets. This is normal and needs to be completed for the probate process to be completed through the court.

Let's use the scenario of a daughter who has been appointed as executor of her mother's estate. You will need to deal directly with the daughter. She may, during this time, have someone come in from auction companies to start giving appraisals on particular items in the house.

I am not going to dwell on the topic of getting these assets liquidated in this chapter; I will discuss this in a later chapter because this likely will be a situation you will encounter. The takeaway for this chapter is, after the appraisal, the probate court is going to confirm the debts claimed.

Maybe the mom who passed away had credit cards with remaining balances or even potential judgments. Maybe she had a car loan. Every debt needs to be confirmed. Once they are confirmed, the assets will be liquidated to satisfy those debts. If mom had a credit card with a $4,000 balance, this debt has to be satisfied before anything can happen with the property. Any debts of any kind against the property, and any debts that are being disputed and held as debts against the property—mortgage/s, tax liens, mechanics liens, etc.—all need to be resolved. This is the part of the process where family issues can rise to the surface. This circumstance is what makes these leads desirable. You are needed to help resolve issues. A lot of individuals don't communicate well. If you can offer your help in this situation, the family members will be glad to have you as a resource.

At times family members have a falling out, yet this must be resolved because decisions need to be made. I would say 80-90% of heirs want to get rid of the property as quickly as possible. The remaining relatives, or heirs, want to split the equity in the property so they can move on and never talk to each other again. This is unfortunate, yet in many cases, the deceased person could have been the string that held everyone together. Now, the remaining relatives left behind want to cut the cord and be done with all contact. No one is there to force the family together. But before that cord can be cut, the process needs to be followed.

Typically, the estate representative or executor will prepare the final report and accounting for submission to the court and beneficiaries according to the will.

Then the executor and the estate representative will distribute the estate according to the will.

At this stage, you can hop in and make an offer on the property to see if you can get it approved. Once you buy the property, and all the debts are completely settled, the case is closed.

Do you see how you can be the missing piece that enables the family to work together?

This is one scenario that can occur, but many situations apply to probate deals. We will talk about all of them. As it pertains to this chapter and building our foundation, we need to talk about the probate elephant in the room, and that is *what if there is no probate process*?

Yes, there are cases where there is no probate on the property. If the deceased set up a living trust for all properties, including the real estate, this property could be passed directly and privately to heirs without the expenses of a probate attorney and executor. This is huge because no other investor will know about this property since it's not been put on public notice like a probate. Even though properties that go through the probate process have minimal investor competition, the avenue of not having to go through the probate means there will be limited to no competition. You won't have to fight with other investors trying to get a deal, which in turn drives up the price and leaves small profit margins.

Depending on the state, the probate process has to go through the legal system, which could take a lot of time potentially. If there was a lot of debt left behind by the deceased, it could tie up the executor of the estate with the outstanding debts. Having a trust set up allows the family to sell the estate quickly without delays and bypasses the probate process. The purchase price also doesn't have to be approved by a judge. This helps expedite the sale. Keep in mind if you can make an offer to the executor of the estate to not only purchase the house but to allow that purchase to help satisfy any outstanding debts left behind by the deceased, it will only speed up the process.

In cases where probates can't be found through traditional marketing methods, and are considered "off-market," you need to ensure that you get yourself in the door with as many investor-friendly attorneys as possible. Investors love off-market properties because they can be purchased quickly at a discount for their own income-producing portfolio if the property is wholesaled and not rehabbed. The properties we put under contract to wholesale are not listed on the Multiple Listing Service (MLS) or any other website advertising homes for sale that makes working directly with us enticing. Since they are not listed, the flood gates open and the contracting properties where heirs have a trust in place flow through, allowing you to bypass liquating assets through the court. This is going to bring up opportunities that a lot of people don't handle correctly. The majority of real estate investors don't want to take the time to establish connections with attorneys. But family members contact these attorneys when settling an estate that doesn't have to go through probate. Once I started connecting with attorneys—especially the ones who set up wills, trusts, and elder law—I received phone calls from heirs as referrals from those attorneys. A living trust, or revocable trust, avoids the probate process and usually leads to assets being distributed faster. When this is the case, you can get a property that has never been listed on the MLS or advertised on any other online publication/website. While others might mishandle this type of deal, you have the advantage since this book is in your hand. You can handle this property correctly to result in a win-win for all parties. Remember, this property is 100% off-market, and in most cases, it is paid off. This means you don't have to worry about paying off any liens, except maybe taxes. This is a highly sought-after property that you definitely want to know how to process.

In most cases, the descendants don't want to worry about the property and will let it go for a low cash offer. I have seen this happen quite often. Even if there is a probate process, a lot of the family members, heirs, and executors, want to get rid of the property as quickly as possible. As I shared with you earlier, this was the case when my grandmother passed.

It was 2005. I could tell my mom, aunt, and uncle all wanted to sell the property quickly. The main reason why was because of the many memories involved in the property, and it was painful. Every time they would walk into the property, those memories would all come flooding back. They were reliving this agony and wanted it to stop. It was even tough for me because I'd lost my grandma yet still had to go back inside her house. Every time I stepped foot in the door, a rush of emotions hit me. I missed her. There was nothing to do but tough it out as I wandered through the rooms and accepted that I would never see her again. Overwhelming emotions is another reason people find it hard to keep a property. This is the reason why most people sell. Sure, there's a very low percentage of people who want to keep the property, yet since this is a slim percentage, it makes acquiring probate properties extremely desirable—especially when you go about it the right way.

Probate Property Types

Regarding residential categorization, probate properties include single-family residences, condos, and townhouses, which could also be called Planned Unit Development (PUD). Manufactured homes are also included in this category, as are mobile homes.

The commercial classification includes the following: multifamily/apartment buildings, vacant industrial lots, self-storage facilities, and anything holding the specific classification of commercial property.

Many properties can be nearly or completely paid off with a treasure trove of personal property, regardless of the classification, so cars, antiques, and collectibles are included.

Once, I was talking to a homeowner while we went through her property.

She just wanted to get rid of the property and all the belongings. We talked about everything involved. Obviously, I didn't want the beds, furniture, or possessions, as these would be a headache for me. When she told me, "Take everything in the house, or we don't have a deal," of course, that condition became part of the contract. After we acquired the property, we trashed the beds and other items that weren't valuable. The main reason I agreed to do the deal this way was because of these little mint antique cars, still wrapped and sealed in their original packaging. They were collectibles. I checked out their value on eBay before I agreed to the terms with the heir. There was close to a hundred of them, and each one was going for $250 to $350 on eBay.

One closet was full of them. I gave a Corvette to my dad because he's a Corvette junkie. We ended up selling those cars for about $150 each. You can do the math. In this case, it was worth it for us to take on the additional property and write it into the deal. Sometimes this is what you need to do to move the contract forward. And sometimes, it will work out, but other times, taking on the property will be a pain in the ass, and you will have to get rid of the old possessions on your dime. If you do, just make sure it makes financial sense before you proceed.

Probate File Contents

These are the items you will find in the probate file.

1. Petition for application for probate.

   This form will give you a lot of information about the deceased and the assets they left behind. These lists are usually created by the executor with assistance from their attorney.

2. Proof of publication. This form contains inventory and appraisement. One of two different types of property appraisals will be done. 1) Either a professional appraiser who drives by and does the appraisal from the car by looking at the property will assess it or 2) a more in-depth appraiser, hired to do a proper appraisal of the property will assess it. Regardless of what appraisal you use, the appraisals are good for one year. In some cases, if the executor has not received an offer to purchase the subject property, the appraisal could come in high, which doesn't allow us to purchase unless the judge grants his/her approval. This is why when you're making your offer, it's important to contact the executor/heirs as soon as possible so you can dodge the bullet of the value coming in too high. Yes, an appraisal will still have to be done, yet having an offer on the table helps you as long as your offer is fair. The judge doesn't want to hold up the family from moving on either, so if a reasonable offer is presented, it'll most likely be approved quickly. Now I don't have a crystal ball and can't give you 100%, a yes or no of what will happen in any of these situations. But as long as the value is within range, the odds are definitely in your favor.

3. Will of the deceased.

4. Notice to creditors.

5. Order for probate.

After you've reviewed the contents in a few of these files, you will notice most of these properties are free and clear.

It still pays to do your due diligence. When you explore a little further, you may find out it's not worth it to proceed because of the number and amount of debts. The good news is when it comes to probates, is that you will also find many of these properties have not been lived in for a while, and the mortgage has been paid off. Dig even more, and if you are lucky, you might also find the property has no liens against it. The point is to gather all the information you can to make the shrewdest deal.

A lot of these properties have been kept up, and that's good news. They also have not been updated, which is also good news, and presents you with an opportunity to put in a little sweat equity, if that's your thing. Believe it or not, a large number of deceased individuals pass on with multiple properties. These could include their primary residence, aka the owner-occupant property, and a second home—classified as a vacation home, as well as others in their portfolio.

One individual left multiple investment properties. Some were rentals, and some lease-to-owns, which also offers opportunities for you to make a nice return.

Descendants usually have no emotional attachment to these other properties, which makes it easier to get them at steep discounts. I recommend examining the probate file to find all the properties owned by the descendant.

6. Inventory and appraisement form.

   This form will give you a list of addresses and the appraised evaluation. This is extremely helpful for you. There will be a record of all the properties on a worksheet that may be governed by different types of wills. This is what you might encounter:

   a. Witness will.

      This is a typewritten legal document dated and signed by both the deceased and witnesses. Sometimes real and personal property is not mentioned in this document. It can also be challenging to find the address in the will due to the property being recorded in the name of a corporation, trust, or LLC.

   b. Holographic will.

      This is a handwritten legal document dated and signed by the deceased. It is not accepted in all states.

   c. Nuncupative will.

      This is an oral will used when very few assets are left behind. Very rarely used, it is also not accepted in all states.

Reading of the Will

When you read the will, do so to pursue the probate, which is limited.

Let me explain.

There will be some legal mumbo jumbo on the paperwork you likely won't understand. Heck, there's stuff I don't understand, and when I encounter this type of information, I know it is meant for the attorneys to manage. After all, they went to school for all those years to practice their specialty. In any case, it's important to know if the deceased did or did not leave real estate behind. You can find this out pretty quickly without much time lost. If there isn't any real estate, then move on to the next individual as there's nothing you can do. Read the will carefully and become familiar with the language. An important element to pay attention to is the testamentary power of a sales statement. In its simplest form, this statement means if the wishes of the deceased are honored, no publication of any kind will be printed except to the creditors. A public notification has to normally be placed in the local newspaper, or it can also appear online on the newspaper company's website. This notice shows the court that a public notice has been given to the creditors.

Properties that are not published have little exposure to the market and can be captured at severe discounts. I highly, highly encourage you to get all the information on the heirs for this reason amongst others. When you do this, you will find out what percentage is going to whom and who has been named the executor. Sometimes, there will be phone numbers and emails listed. The majority of the time, there will be a physical address for the executors and the descendants of the actual will. As you flip through this file, the final piece of paper should be the notice to the creditors and includes outstanding credit cards, car loans, IRS taxes, judgments, installment loans, etc.

These debts are sent to the descendants who may have an equitable interest in the estate. If you have a rock-solid foundation for this probate property, you will have a leg up over the competition in your area.

You're also going to have a leg up because you now know how to start systematizing. And when you can do this, you will not only stay organized; you will know exactly what to look out for and what makes for a good deal. Wasn't that simple? And you gained such an edge already by reading one single chapter!

I'm looking forward to giving you more information in our upcoming chapters and getting you one step closer to closing your first probate deal.

CHAPTER TWO: FORMS OF PROPERTY OWNERSHIP

It's important to have an attorney who understands how you, as a real estate investor, will be diving into purchasing properties directly from the heirs' properties who've just lost a loved one. I've known my attorney Matthew Griffith since 2009, and I quickly understood that working together with Matt on anything I needed legally as a real estate investor would help me out dramatically. The guy is a wealth of knowledge, and he's helped a ton when navigating through complicated processes that only an attorney would understand how to execute.

When I first hired Matt, I had him review all my paperwork to make sure I was operating legally. As our relationship grew and he understood my business model he gave me recommendations based on where I wanted to go as an investor. I asked him to write a chapter in *Flipping Out Over Probates* because I'm not an attorney, and he's the best in the business when it comes to giving insights on all the legal stuff you need to know. Anyone who has attended any of our seminars over the years knows when Matt speaks, he over-delivers every single time. The next few paragraphs will be in Matt's words, so I'm giving you a heads up right now that you should change your Snuggies because it's about to get crazy.

When a property owner dies, there is always a change in ownership. That is even true when there are two or more owners. So, for example, if a husband and wife own a home, as joint tenants when the husband dies, the wife automatically becomes the new owner. Or, as another example, when that same wife, now a widow, passes away, the home will pass on to someone else. But, the nature of the property interests that pass on depends on two key factors. First, you need to determine how the deceased owner held the title. Second, you need to determine whether the deceased owner's property interests passed through a deed, trust, the last will, or intestate. In this chapter, we will explore the different scenarios by which title can pass.

In other words, relevant to this book on acquiring properties through the probate process, you might discover other non-probate ways to make money assisting in the transfer of ownership interests from a deceased person to the next owner. In simple terms, probate is not the only game in town. And if you have a more comprehensive understanding of how people own real estate and how title transfers on death, you will have more tools and skillsets to identify opportunities and maximize your profits.

This chapter serves another benefit because you, too, will eventually die. When you do, assuming you own real estate at the time of your death, you will want to control how your real estate passes on to your intended beneficiaries. If you do not understand the nature of your ownership interests or you do not understand the tools by which your ownership interests in real property will pass, you are less likely to satisfy your estate planning goals. Ignorance is not bliss. But knowledge is power. The more knowledge you have about the different types of ownership and the tools to transfer that ownership, the more control you have to effectuate your estate planning goals.

Let's start with some basic real property law concepts. First, we'll outline the different ways that someone can hold title to real estate. Although these basic concepts will apply to nearly all states in the US, there will be variations on state laws, from state to state, which will impact these basic concepts. As always, check with a knowledgeable and seasoned real estate lawyer or an estate planning lawyer to determine if these concepts apply in your state. That said, here are the basic forms of ownership:

- *Sole owner using a simple deed to hold title*
- *Tenants in common*
- *Joint tenants*
- *Tenants by the entireties*
- *Life estate*
- *Land contract purchaser (also known as a buyer under contract for deed)*

In exploring these concepts in more detail, we find that, unfortunately, there is no other way to master these concepts than to study them. So, while this section of this chapter might not be sexy, fun, or funny, you will be glad you studied these important legal concepts. And you will be a better real estate investor for having done so.

Sole Owner Using a Simple Deed to Hold Title

The simplest and most common form of ownership is when one person acquires the title to real estate through a deed. By way of example, let's assume a young man named Allen graduates from college, gets a great job, saves money for a down payment, and purchases a small cottage home. When Allen buys the home, he receives a deed. The deed, presumably a warranty deed, causes ownership interests to transfer from Allen's seller to Allen.

There may be liens and encumbrances impacting Allen's title, such as his mortgage and possibly restrictive covenants for his neighborhood association, but Allen owns the house. He is the fee simple titleholder. He is also the mortgagor, and his bank is the mortgagee.

If nothing else changes, on Allen's death, his interests in the house will transfer to his heirs. In a section below in this chapter, we will discuss the different ways that Allen's interests in his home will transfer to his heirs. For now, keep in mind that one person owning one parcel of real estate as the full titleholder is the simplest and purest form of real estate ownership.

Tenants in Common

Tenants in common comprise two or more persons who own a parcel of real estate together. Notice that I did not use the word "jointly." There is a related or similar concept to tenancy in common, called "Joint Tenancy." "Tenants in Common" have different rights and responsibilities than do persons owning real estate as "Joint Tenants." For the purposes of this book, the main difference between tenancy in common vs. joint tenancy is in what happens to your ownership interests on death. Under tenancy in common, the other owner or owners do not inherit the ownership interests of the co-owner if the co-owner dies.

Let's assume for a moment our friend Allen decides to buy a horse farm with his sister Carol. Neither Allen nor Carol are lawyers or are wise enough to hire a lawyer. They go to an office supply store and purchase a pre-printed deed form. Unbeknownst to Allen or Carol, the deed form they select creates a tenancy in common. Perhaps this is what Allen and Carol desired. Or, they were lucky to pick the right deed form. As a result of selecting a tenancy in common deed forum, Allen and Carol are tenants in common.

Consequently, when Carol becomes ill and suddenly passes away, pursuant to her last will, Carol's husband acquires Carol's interests in the horse farm. Now, after Carol passes away, Allen and Carol's widower are tenants in common. Allen never liked Carol's husband and certainly never wanted to own anything along with Carol's widower. But because Allen and Carol selected a tenancy in common deed form and made no arrangements to deal with an early death of either of them, Allen is now stuck with his brother-in-law as a co-owner.

To make matters worse for Allen, Carol owned 65% of the horse farm, meaning Carol's widower now owns 65%. This leaves Allen as a minority owner relative to a guy he doesn't like. There are other consequences to owning property as tenants-in-common without written agreements to address things like access, use, and enjoyment of the property, taxes, insurance, maintenance, and other expenses. For purposes of this book, what is relevant is the manner in which Carrol's interests transferred to her husband on her death.

Of course, as stated above, the tenancy in common concept is often confused with joint tenancy.

Joint Tenants

In simple terms, joint tenants have rights of survivorship. This means that upon the death of a joint tenant, the other joint tenants acquire the ownership interests of the person who just passed away. Let's apply this concept to Allen and Carol, assuming for a moment they bought the farm as joint tenants. Under this scenario, if Carrol passes away, her 65% ownership of the horse farm would automatically be acquired by Allen. This is good for Allen, yet not so good for Carol's widower or their three young children. And, assume that Carol (and her widower) borrowed $80,000 from her home equity line of credit to buy the horse farm with Allen. That means Carol's widower is stuck with an $80,000 debt on his home, and Allen walks off with the horse farm.

As you can see, there are advantages and disadvantages to the various ways to hold title. Most people do not take the time to make the right choices in structuring their affairs. Unfortunately, there are real consequences to making mistakes in acquiring and holding title to real property.

Tenants by the Entireties

Another form of joint tenancy is called "Tenants by the Entireties," which is joint tenancy of a property by only a husband and wife. There are only about 13 states that recognize tenants by the entireties. Readers in two-thirds of the US will not have this form of ownership available to them. However, many investors purchase property in another state from where they live. Consequently, if you are purchasing property in a state that recognizes tenants by the entireties, this is a concept you should understand.

Before I explain this concept in any more detail, let me discuss an issue that is not yet resolved. Specifically, most of the states that recognize Tenants by the entireties have state statutes that define tenants by the entireties as husband and wife. However, many states now recognize same-sex marriages. Traditionally, the term "husband" refers to a man, and the term "wife" refers to a woman. I am unaware of any case law determining whether a same-sex couple may hold property as tenants by the entireties. So far, the courts that have looked at state rights that apply to same-sex couples have extended state rights to those same-sex couples, rather than invalidating the state laws that grant rights. In other words, so far, the courts have given same-sex couples the same rights as heterosexual couples, rather than invalidating state statutes creating rights. I am of the opinion that, sooner or later, the courts will recognize same-sex couples as having rights to hold title to real estate as tenants by the entireties. I feel that the courts will not invalidate Tenants by the entireties, simply because the state statutes refer to husband and wife rather than the term spouse.

With that particular issue aside, the concept of estates by the entireties, for purposes of this book, is essentially the same as joint tenancy. In other words, joint tenants are joint tenants, whether they are married or not. If one tenant dies, the other tenants shared the deceased tenant's ownership percentage.

In most states that recognize tenants by the entireties, the courts will treat a deed containing the husband's and wife's names as creating a tenancy by the entireties. If, for example, John and Cindy are married and buy a home together with both of their names appearing on the deed, that creates a tenancy by the entireties. Presumably, if, for example, Mike and Josh, two men who are married at the time, purchase a property together with both of their names appearing on the deed, the courts might treat that as a deed creating a tenancy by the entireties. This issue is not yet resolved at the time this chapter was written. But going back to John and Cindy for a moment, it is safe to say that the deed naming John and Cindy as co-owners would create a tenancy by the entireties if their state recognizes that form of ownership.

If John and Cindy get a divorce, the tenancy by the entireties converts to joint tenancy. The tenancy by the entireties is only available while John and Cindy are married. If John dies while still married to Cindy, Cindy automatically becomes the sole owner. Cindy will then need to file a document with the County Recorder explaining that John has passed away and that the Tenants by the entireties has dissolved. That document is called a "survivor's affidavit" or sometimes "affidavit of survivorship." Often, investors will need to have a survivor execute and record a survivor's affidavit before that survivor can transfer title to the investor. The survivor's affidavit cleans up the official title record.

Life Estate

A life estate is a form of ownership, by which a person has the right to live in and occupy a property while they are alive. Upon death, the life estate ends. Normally, legal title is held in one person's name, and the life estate is held in a different person's name. For example, Bill might buy his mother's home, subject to a life estate in her favor. That means Bill is the legal titleholder, but his mother has all equitable title. Bill would be responsible for paying the taxes and insuring the property, and possibly maintaining it as well, while his mother has the right to live there. If done properly, there will be a deed or some other document that is recorded which describes and defines the life estate. There are difficult cases involving undocumented and unrecorded life estates. Again, this legal concept is not often properly implemented because people use bad legal documents. However, this is a common form of split ownership and is an important concept that investors should keep in mind.

Land Contract Purchaser (also known as a Contract for Deed)

A land contract purchaser is someone who is making installment payments, or possibly a lump sum or "balloon" to acquire the title to real estate. Legal title is held by the seller, while the buyer holds equitable title. In most states, a land contract is treated as a note and mortgage, with the seller serving the role of the bank. The seller essentially is treated by the courts as a mortgage lender, which must go through a long, expensive, and difficult foreclosure process to get possession and title of a property back from a buyer who has defaulted. Many land contract sellers attempt to avoid the state foreclosure laws by drafting favorable contract language. Specifically, sellers will draft land contracts that grant the seller the right to forfeiture, rather than foreclosure. Unfortunately for sellers, most courts in most states hold that those contract provisions granting the seller forfeiture rights are unenforceable. In other words, sellers cannot evict a land contract buyer and are forced to go through the foreclosure process, which ends with a sheriff's foreclosure sale.

Sometimes, a land contract is not recorded. That scenario poses real risks to investors, because they may not realize they are buying a property that is subject to a land contract. The chances of this scenario happening increase when the land contract seller dies, and his family is unaware of the land contract. I have seen more than a few times situations in which a land contract buyer attempts to purchase real estate—usually a home that is already being purchased by a land contract buyer. This is where good contracts and title insurance come into play. What is important for the purposes of this book is that investors understand the impact of both recorded and unrecorded land contracts.

There are a few other more exotic forms of real estate ownership, but the concepts discussed above represent the most common scenarios that investors will face. It is important that investors study and learn much more about how these concepts and the different types of deeds are used to transfer and hold title to real estate. Now let's take a look at the four most common ways that title transfers to real estate upon someone's death.

Transfers by Deeds

We have already discussed above a couple of ways that a deed can transfer the title to real estate. As explained, in most states, title to real estate transfers automatically occur upon a person's death if that person held title with other people as joint tenants. Generally, transfers from one joint tenant to one or more other joint tenants happen automatically on death. The survivor's affidavit discussed above merely tells the world that title transferred. There is no requirement that a will be probated, or a trust administered, where there is joint tenancy. Transfers by joint tenancy occur whether a person died with or without a will or trust.

There is another way that title can transfer automatically upon a person's death through the impact of a deed. In about 13 states, a person can automatically transfer property at death to another person through a "transfer on death" deed (sometimes referred to as a "TOD Deed"). This is not the same arrangement as joint tenancy. For example, we'll assume Seth owns a property under a TOD deed, and that deed states that Seth's oldest daughter will acquire title to the property immediately on Seth's death. Seth's daughter does not own the property as a joint tenant or a tenant-in-common with Seth. In fact, she holds no ownership interest in the property until Seth dies. However, the moment Seth passes away, title to the real estate passes to his daughter. Again, as is the case of joint tenancy, Seth's daughter will need to record a survivor's affidavit to tell the world that her father has passed away and that the title to the real estate now belongs to her.

The TOD deed is a tool that can be used by tenants in common and even a surviving joint tenant. For example, let's assume for a moment that Seth owns real estate as tenants in common with his brother, Phil. If Seth and Phil used a TOD deed, and Seth passes away, Seth's ownership interests would automatically transfer to his daughter. The property can then be owned by Phil and Seth's daughter as tenants in common. As you might imagine, a skilled real estate or estate planning attorney can use combinations of all these tools to transfer property from one person to another based upon the owner's wishes. These tools are also used in conjunction with a last will or a trust. Before we turn our attention to the two most common estate planning tools, the last will, and the trust, we should take a look at intestate.

Intestate

Intestate simply means dying without a last will or trust. A person who dies intestate has no direct control over the distribution of their assets at death. Now, that might not be a big deal if that person uses other tools to control when, how, and to whom assets are distributed. For example, a transfer on death deed is a fantastic tool to transfer assets, specifically real estate, to another person at death without the need for a last will or trust. So, a great deal of estate planning can be done without a last will or a trust. Dying intestate does not mean that a person does not have a plan. It simply means that we need to look closer to determine what other planning tools that person might have used to transfer assets to loved ones.

Last Will

A last will often called the "Last Will & Testament," is a legal instrument, executed with certain formalities, that typically directs the disposition of a person's property at death. The advantages of a will are that they are easily changed and revoked and are great for younger people who are still buying and selling assets—who will make changes over the years and who might need to create testamentary trusts or pick guardians for minor children.

Because of the many advantages of wills, they are common. Other planning tools, like trusts and the TOD deed, are becoming more popular. There are, however, a huge number of estates governed by a will. Keep in mind that a will only controls real property that was in the deceased person's name at the time of death. So, if the deceased person used a TOD deed, had joint owners, or placed the property in a trust, they will not impact how that property transfers after death.

Trusts

A trust is a fiduciary relationship in which a trustee holds legal title to specific property under a fiduciary duty to manage, invest, safeguard, and administer the trust assets and income for the benefit of designated beneficiaries, who hold equitable title. The advantages of a trust are that we can avoid the slow, frustrating, and expensive probate process. Trusts generally are preferred by older people who do not intend to alter their asset portfolio, who want privacy, and who want to leave specific items or sums of money for specific persons. Over the past 30 years, largely as a result of marketing by estate planning lawyers, trusts have become more popular.

For our purposes, there are three kinds of trusts-

- *Testamentary Trust- This is a trust created inside a last will. Typically, a deed to real estate will be held in the name of the deceased person, and then must be transferred to the trust after death. So, probate could be required to get a title transferred to the testamentary trust.*
- *Living Trust- This is a trust that is live and active immediately upon its creation. But, a parcel of real estate is not officially in the trust until a deed is executed to transfer title to the trust. Often, people will use a tool called a "Pour-Over Will," which*

causes all assets at death, which are not already in a trust, to be transferred to the trust. Again, probate and a deed might be required to get a title transferred to the trust.

- *Land Trust- A land trust is probably the most misunderstood and inappropriately used real estate investing tool ever created. In simple terms, a land trust merely transfers legal title from the owner to a surrogate titleholder. For example, Johnny creates a land trust and executes a deed from him to the "Red River Land Trust," naming his friend Butch as the trustee. Johnny still owns the property, but Johnny's name no longer appears on title. Johnny holds all equitable title. A land trust creates limited anonymity for Johnny, but no estate planning benefits and no asset protection. Many land trusts are disguised to appear to be living trusts, which means you need to read the trust documents carefully to determine what kind of trust is at play.*

Who Am I Dealing With?

Before you can cut a deal to buy a property after someone has died, you must first determine what you're buying and from whom. This can get complicated, but you can use this chapter as a reference source to help diagnose the situation. Let me give you an example of how important it is to correctly identify who owns what when you're trying to do a deal after someone has passed away.

I had an investor client call me once with this fact pattern. The investor was working with the niece of a man (Albert) who had just died. Albert had owned a house with his sister Monica. Monica was my client's aunt. Monica had owned and lived in this house with Albert, as tenants in common. Monica left her half of the house to my client. Albert dies without a will or trust, or any children of his own. So, through intestate law, Albert's half ownership of the house went to my client equally with his eight cousins. After Albert died, two of those cousins died, meaning there were other heirs. In the end, 11 people owned half of this house.

What a nightmare!

My client began the process of negotiating to buy her cousins' interests but never could get deeds from all her cousins, several of whom wanted to be paid a lot of money to relinquish their interests in the house. Eventually, my client may become the owner, under the doctrine of Adverse Possession, because she is living in the house and paying the taxes, but an investor cannot currently purchase this house. There are too many owners, and those owners do not agree on how to treat the house. And this is, unfortunately, an increasingly common scenario. At least five clients have come to me with eight or more second and third-generation owners of a single home. These are difficult cases to resolve, and usually, there is too much work for an investor. Go find lower hanging fruit. Equally important, in the very beginning, do your title research to determine who owns a house. Far too often, investors waste weeks or months working on a deal, only to learn later that good clean title cannot be transferred. Don't waste your time. Confirm ownership fast. If you can't confirm ownership, move on to another deal.

Conclusion:
What Does This All Mean to Me as an Investor?

If you're going to play a game, you need to know the rules. Before you play chess, you first have to learn how each piece moves on the board. Before you can develop a strategy or learn tactics (moves to further a strategy), you have to understand the basics-the rules. The better you understand the rules, the more likely you are to control your strategy, implement your tactics, read your opponent's moves, and win. Having a command of the rules is critical to winning any game.

Investing in real estate is not a game; it's serious business. But just like playing chess or any game really, you cannot expect to win if you do not fully and completely understand the rules of investing. That means you must understand how title is held and transferred at death if you want to be an investor who helps property transfer from a deceased person to the next owner. It is virtually impossible to be a "probate investor," if you don't understand the probate process. And if you don't understand that most real property transfers at death OUTSIDE of the formal probate process, then you are really at a disadvantage if you do not master the concepts outlined in this chapter.

On the other hand, if you take this chapter as an introduction to your education on these topics and you study, read and learn more about deeds, wills, trusts, and probate, then you are going to do better than most probate investors. You will be able to identify opportunities, avoid pitfalls, and maximize profits. Master these concepts, and you'll be a wiser and richer investor.

For more information about Matthew Griffith, and free resources, make sure to check out his website. He can be found here: www.IndyBizLaw.com.

CHAPTER THREE: KEEP BUILDING

We laid the foundation for probates in chapter one and discussed crucial information you need to understand to ensure you get clear titles in chapter two. Now we're going to continue to build on that basis so you can move forward and start seeing the results you want within your business. Because when you start implementing this strategy for finding and flipping probate properties, and you do it by executing the exact steps in this book, you are going to set yourself apart. You will start to receive the types of deals you want to get under contract at the prices that will enable you to flip massively at great profits.

What hurts the majority of entrepreneurs is the lack of a plan to move forward with any element of their business. A lot of entrepreneurs tend to over-analyze, over-think, and even over-read. Yes, as the author of this book, it might be weird to read that, but I do not want you to read this book three, four, or five times. As much as I would love to know you're reading my book that voraciously, I also know this will not be helpful to you. If, after reading this book once, you still aren't grasping the information with enough confidence to move forward, please re-read it. If you need additional guidance, don't hesitate to reach out to us at support@jasonlucchesi.com, and we'll be more than happy to lend you a hand. I want you to feel confident in knowing what you're going to be doing yet diving into the content over and over again would be overkill. That said, once you are done with the book, keep it handy. You can still pick it up and read it from time to time. I always find going through a refresher helps. We all forget what we've learned, so don't be afraid to crack this sucker open and take advantage of the tips, tricks, and selling strategies periodically. You can apply them to enhance your business and create the consistency you want in your business.

The promise I want you to make is that you are not going to spend too much time with your nose in this book. Go out there and make it happen. Go out there and start networking. Go out there and build your business. Make money. That's the whole point of this book.

With all the knowledge I'm dropping on you right now, you can have your business set up virtually; that's just one part of the plan which I will get to later. For now, just know that no matter what part of the business we're talking about, I always make a plan. That's what I want you to take away, too, and then I encourage you to do the same. I also always make a quarterly plan for myself, so I can see where I would be if I hit my goals. Then once I get there, I can determine if I've exceeded what I wanted to do, or if I made the goals harder on myself. It's really valuable to your business to take the extra time to assess where you landed with your goals. Then you can adjust where you are aiming. Maybe you need to level up and shoot higher? If you didn't meet your goals, then you know it's time to recalculate what you need to do. Whether you hit your goal or not, you still need to take a pulse of what you should do, what you did, and what else you want to do. You should know how you performed or not. This gives you the information you need, so your steps are planned. And when your steps are well-thought-out and anticipated, I don't have to tell you they will also be surer.

Here's what I want you to do moving forward in your business.

Mission Statement

Write up your mission statement. It's important to do. Not just for yourself, but it benefits people who are going to be on your team. Maybe the contractors working with you would like to read it to get a clearer picture of what your goals are. And then there are the people you haven't even identified yet, who will be a part of your team. Reading your mission statement will help them in the work they will be doing for you. People want to know more about you and your company even if they aren't on your team. At some point in time, you might want to have a website or a Facebook business page. Regardless of where you put it or how you distribute it, you must have a public mission statement.

If you don't know where to start to create a mission statement, this next section will help you.

Your "Why"

But before you read any further, I want you to ask yourself, *why am I doing real estate*? (Your answer doesn't necessarily need to be anything about probate.) When you are thinking about what you want to say, consider that there are reasons other than money to get involved in real estate investing. I don't want your answer to just be about money. Money is simply an object. Money brings opportunities to you. And I don't want to devolve into a motivational or inspirational speech here either. That's not what this book is about, even though I could absolutely get you fired up and motivated in that way. The point is, I know you have a deeper reason defining the pull inside you to get into this business. So, what is it?

I promise you at the end of this book, you will have everything you need to go out there and successfully work in this business, but you've got to take the steps along the way before you race to the end of the line and work the deals. If you don't, you're just going through the motions, and that's another thing I am confident about: you will go nowhere in building your business if you rush through taking in the knowledge you need. I've been in this business a while and have had time to observe behavior. Most people fail because they don't have a business plan set up. They don't have a plan to move forward. They don't know what is propelling them to want to work in the business in the first place.

Think about it like this. Imagine you want to take a cruise from Miami, Florida to the Bahamas (even though I'm not a fan of cruise ships because I get bad motion sickness). What's going to happen if the captain does not have a charted path? You're going to go all over the place. When you embark on this crazy route, you'll have no idea how long it's supposed to take to get from Miami to the Bahamas on a cruise liner. Now, let's assume it takes one day to get there on a charted path. Unlucky for you, the captain didn't have a charted path, and he took five days to get there. That's how a lot of people operate within their businesses. They don't have a charted path to get from one step to the next, and they wind up all over the place. They wind up in places that are hard to get out of. Put your mission statement together so you will have a clearer understanding of what you want to do. What is your objective? Do you know your "why" yet?

We just finished up a conference not too long ago. When we do a conference, helping people figure out their "why" is high on our list. This is critical to know because it ties into every action you take. So carve out some time to determine what this is for you. For a lot of folks, it's spending time with their family. Having money is an opportunity to increase family time, go on vacations together, or maybe buy that bigger home you wanted, which will allow everyone to have their own space—as you all enjoy more family space. What you want to do is not just about cars, cash, or material things. Even though those are great, don't get me wrong; I'm not knocking anybody wanting a nice car or watch. There's nothing wrong with wanting nice stuff. Just like there's nothing wrong with giving your money away if you want to. Some people are hell-bent on giving to charities. If this is you, cool. We love giving, too, and knowing your "why" will help you hit your goals so you can get nice stuff for yourself as you give to charities.

Your Action Steps: "Plan, Do, Check, Adjust"

The next part of your business plan is to create a list of action steps. These are steps you will take to meet and exceed your business goals. Let's say, for example; you're putting together your buyer's list. After you did that, you would focus on finding probate deals. Then, you would create systemization and develop your exit strategy. (BTW, I share with you in the later chapters some ultra-juicy exit strategies you can use within your business—so don't miss them.) Next, you will put together your cash buyer's list.

This is important because you can't work any of the deals I am going to tell you about without it.

Regarding systemization, if you're running your business solo, you will need to know how every process works. The only way to scale and move your business to the next level is by eliminating yourself from being in the business. You can do this by creating processes. When you do, you can work on the business while other people work the processes. Scaling is the only way your business can grow.

You and I both know there are only 24 hours in a day. If you are the only person on your team, then you only have so much time in your day to accomplish your goals. But if you start building and scaling with a team, then you're going to be able to use and value more of your own time as you create more opportunities for your entire team. When you reach that point, I can't stress enough how monumental that will be for you...and everyone on your team!

Once your team's roles and responsibilities are established, and you know your roles in scaling, it's time to establish your target market. What are your buyers interested in? It's a short question and doesn't seem complex, but this is a question you will continue to ask yourself frequently as we cruise through these chapters and even as you continue to operate your business over the years. This is information you need to keep your finger on. You need to know if your buyers are not looking in your target market. If that is the case, then either get new buyers or reevaluate your market.

When you're creating your 90-day business plan, I like to use a process called "Plan, Do, Check, Adjust." You can give yourself a huge leg-up in business when you establish a plan

A, to make sure there is no plan B. Before you read any further before you work on another item in your business, accept that there is no Plan B. It's gone. Get it out of your head right now. The ship for plan B has completely sunk (on that uncharted cruise). You only have a plan A. You must make plan A work.

Your plan A is your "Do, Check, Adjust." To break down what I mean: you make a plan; you check it, and when you need to adjust it, you can. "Adjust" is part of the plan, so that step is truly okay. Where a person's path gets rough is when they don't do that last part and refuse to adjust the plan. Instead, they focus on what *doesn't work*, and they keep pounding away at it *knowing it's not working.* Don't let that be you. Don't be afraid to adjust the plan.

I know you're not one of those people who keeps trying to shove the square peg in the round hole. You're reading this book right now, and for that, I applaud you. So, before you gloss over what I've just told you, tell yourself you will adjust your plan if need be. Work on seeing what isn't meeting your goals and then adjust fire so you can hit them. This is what I always coach our students to do.

Now, it's time to write out your business goal, and you are going to get very specific here. Let's say the goal is, "I want to add 12 new cash buyers to my investor VIP database." That's a great start!

But you still have work to do. You need to get the "hows" answered.

Three Examples of How To Phrase Your "Hows"

1. "Contact 10 new cash buyers daily through Craigslist. This includes reaching out to rented properties with a property manager I can speak with." (Insider tip: contact the property manager. Because what do property managers manage? Properties. Of course, they will have access to people buying properties. AND...they would love to do a deal with you, which could result in them receiving a joint venture fee.)

2. "Contact 10 new investor-friendly real estate agents daily, that could help me review properties which have recently sold for cash." Now, we're going to review more of this in later chapters, but do you understand why it is important to evaluate deals that have sold for cash...especially in the areas where you're going to be doing business? You need to know what properties investors are looking for, meaning the style of house they will want.

   Maybe they want a three-bedroom, one-bath. I use this property type as an example because those will comprise the majority of the properties selling in that particular neighborhood (wherever you happen to be looking and assessing). Now, I'm not saying the majority of the properties are always going to be like that, because we have investors who love three-bedroom, one-bathroom homes, and they also like two-bedroom, one-and-a-half baths because they're easy to get rented out.

3. "Contact five new investor-friendly title companies that can refer me to investors they know closing on properties with all cash." Referrals of title companies can come from other wholesalers, attorneys, property managers, real estate agents, insurance brokers, or by doing a simple Google search. You need to know who you need for your team. Now, not all of these people you can use for two-way referrals are going to be folks you'll add right away. If you are an individual who already has a team, great, but you may need others, you haven't anticipated on your team, too. You might need a property acquisitions and liquidations manager right off the bat. This is someone who is also sometimes called a liquidations and disposition manager. The terms are interchangeable.

Who You Need

Property Acquisitions and Liquidation Manager

Adding the property acquisitions and liquidation manager will allow you to keep the stream of deals coming in while your current deals are closing without issues. Because let's face it, you shouldn't be going to closings and collecting checks. You should be allowing your team to get the deals closed virtually and receiving bank wires. The individuals who receive checks and post them on Facebook are great, especially if those checks are coming from the first two deals. Anything after that is a little excessive. Be a business professional. Once the deal is closed, move on, invest, and continue to do your business. There's no need to snap a pic of any additional checks. Keep your focus where it needs to be.

Title Company & Attorney

When you close, you're going to need to get title insurance on your first transaction, and that means you will need a title company. As we start going over exit strategies in later chapters, you're going to understand why choosing a solid title company is so important. You're going to need to ensure a clear title on the property, so it's critical that you get the title company lined up. Or if you're in an attorney state, meaning you have to close with an attorney, you need to have a clear title on the property. You don't want to close with any clouds on the title or any discrepancies. A cloud on the title could mean the deceased forgot to pay a credit card, and now a judgment is appearing on the title, and it must be paid before closing. Some other examples of what clouds on titles represent are federal/state tax lien, municipality lien, second/third mortgage, mechanics lien, debt collections that have turned into judgments, and code violations, etc. Just picture any outstanding debt owed on the property, which can be turned into a lien against the property and can cause major issues with the title—that makes it defective. You must always close on properties knowing 100% of the time the title is free and clear.

Buyers, Private Lenders & JV Partners

Next, line up connections to buyers, private money, and JV partners. When my partners and I needed to secure private money, a title company helped us out. Private money lenders that have been recommended from our title companies have helped individuals we've established relationships with that are looking to make money because they're failing right now on the stock market. People fall on hard times periodically, and their earnings take a dip. Then they're not making money. Or, maybe they don't have enough money in the bank. Private money lenders are helpful people to keep in your back pocket so you can get deals with these mitigating circumstances closed.

We've done several deals since we have networked with JV partners. Through these avenues, we have been able to find other legitimate cash buyers who have been completely vetted out because they're already closing transactions at the title company. Wouldn't you love to have a referral source send you those types of people doing that type of business? Well, you can work with a title company. I'll recommend where to find title companies later in this chapter.

Real Estate Agent

Your next step is to line up a knowledgeable and dependable real estate agent. A real estate agent worth their salt can get you accurate comps using the multiple listing service, aka the MLS. They can help you fill out purchase and sales agreements. If you're brand new to this gig, the best thing I would encourage you to do is use your state-approved purchase and sales agreements. Your real estate agent can give these to you. They can also access the listed estate sale and probate properties for you.

Because they can give you this access, this gives you an enormous advantage. Sure, you might be able to find something off the MLS, and you might be able to make some offers that originated from there as well. If you're thinking: *well, if nobody's making offers on those properties, then why don't I do that*? You are reading my mind.

Here's a scenario: what if a property is listed for $80,000, you know you could get it for $40,000, and then do a quick wholesale for $50,000? Would it be worth it for you to make $10,000 off a deal nobody else was bidding on? I would think so. I would think you would be nodding right now as you're reading the book—regardless of whether that property originated from the MLS or not.

You've Got Your Team. Now, It's Time to Move!

If you want to maximize your investment, it is important to move quickly on these deals before they get too much exposure. This is where a great agent comes in. If you have a really good agent who can set up these quick searches for you and update you daily, you could say, "Hey Joe Schmo Realtor, I need to make an offer on this property."

How quickly you move has almost nothing to do with how fast you can see the property. I always tell folks that we hardly ever see our properties in person. Wholesalers just don't need to. Yes, we see them from time to time, but I hardly ever see them. The team sometimes wants to go and see the properties, but this isn't a necessity for you or me. One of the best ways to get around this involves dealing with a cash buyer. Before long, I will tell you my secrets for handling this phase of the process. I want you to know that we're in this together.

I want you not only to read this book because the subject interests you but also to take away as much information as you can so you can see the results you desire.

Connecting with Cash Buyers

Speaking of desire, sometimes, what you want the most in a deal will be blocked by an obstacle. Here's a common issue that arises as a flipper. Say, for instance, you're on vacation out of the state. That's okay! You should be allowed to take a vacation. You should be encouraged to enjoy your life from the fruits of your labor. All you do in this situation is let your cash buyers know where you will be and that you need them to pinch-hit for you. Maybe you would send off the property in question to three or four exclusive individuals that you know will make a decision very quickly. These are professionals you've done business with previously, and you know you can count on them, or you know they can close because of their reputation in the community. The real estate investor community is small, and you'll figure out who the good guys/gals are pretty quickly just by asking around. Heck, you can be brand-new at this and never have closed a deal before and still find people who will help you for the right reasons. In any regard, make sure the folks you're dealing with have been vetted, which we'll discuss in detail in a later chapter.

You could say the following to a potential buyer: "Hi Victor. This is Jason. I just wanted to let you know I came across a really great property that we got under contract. I'm not able to see the interior of the property. So I'm putting it at a solid price to get rid of it as quickly as possible and get it in the hands of somebody like yourself who will get this property rehabbed and back on the market. You can make a ton of money from this deal. We're selling it as-is and at a rock bottom price. If you would like to move forward on it, let me know before the end of the day. I am sending this property off to three other people, as well, and I do anticipate this property will move quickly. Thank you for your consideration, Jason."

Go ahead and rip off, then customize my words and use them either in email, a text, over the phone or through a social media DM, etc. You don't have to look at the property either. Just send somebody on your team or maybe a real estate agent to put a lockbox on the house—as long as you get permission from the homeowner—then you're good to go. If you're not able to find an agent, you can always acquire this license yourself. If you already have one, then you have an edge since you have access to the MLS.

It is not necessary to get this license (I don't have one) since you can connect with an investor-friendly realtor. I've always been the type of person who likes to network with folks and build relationships. As a result, I've been able to gain access to the MLS as a non-licensed sales assistant, which you can do as well. If you have an agent you have a really good relationship with, they can always add you as a non-licensed sales assistant and agree to pay the fee for it. Obviously, you want to reimburse them for the fee, which is normally about $350. But paying it will give you complete and total access to the MLS. When you have unrestricted access to this site, you can do your comps much more quickly. Bonus!

Locate Your People

Believe it or not, one of the best places to look for a title company or an attorney is LinkedIn. If you're in an attorney-close state, go on LinkedIn, and type in the search engine in the upper left-hand corner "escrow officer attorney." Naturally, you can also type in "title company," and it'll pull up title companies. Once you get the results, look for people in those areas. You don't want companies; you want people. So, go to filters and enter the specific area where you want to find these people. Depending on what you entered, you can find the types of people you want. Even if the area is smaller, you can still find who you are looking for to help you.

If you have established a reputable network, then you might not need to look very far to find who you are seeking. Good word of mouth from individuals within your sphere goes a long way and carries a lot of weight. If you don't have a sphere of influence of individuals, I would recommend working on building one up. If the prospect of this intimidates you, don't worry. We're going to talk about how to grow your network in later chapters.

If you are curious about how to find a real estate agent who has the chops to handle your deals, here's a simple trick. Go on to Zillow. Use their agent finder within your area and start recruiting real estate agent-friendly individuals for your team. You can find real estate agents on Facebook, too. But there's a trick to finding agents this way. The motherlode of real estate agents can be found within groups. Here's the hack. In Facebook, type in "real estate Indianapolis" or "real estate" wherever you live, "Minneapolis," "Austin," etc.

When you search for groups this way, you can pull up all of the individual groups within your particular area. Everybody has groups specifically tied to those areas. So, it's easier than you think to connect with real estate agents on Facebook. You just need a few tricks up your sleeve.

Of course, you can do the same exact thing on LinkedIn. Searching for these people on social media is simple, and when you use the tactics, I teach you, it works. Think about how you can really set yourself apart as a business professional when you can find the right types of people to contribute to your super-strong team. Choosing reliable players for your team helps you to create a powerful sphere of influence that you can then use to capture what you need. The best part about it all? The help goes both ways.

Remember, as you go through each chapter to make sure you are implementing new tactics and strategies from what you've learned.

As you're reading through this book, if you experience even one "aha" moment, make sure you write it down. For some of you who are newer to making probate deals, make sure you jot down as many insights as possible. Write down what you need to know to revisit the specific information you need. If you need to come back to a particular page or chapter, write down the page you might need a little bit more reading time on. Don't spend time reading the entire book because you have work to do! Maybe just jot down, "I need to go over this page again," so you can access it again and then shortcut the process to implement what you have learned as quickly as possible.

The main purpose of this book is to get you as much information as possible. I want to make sure I explain what is needed to flip deals in the best way without the fluff successfully. So, if there is a little bit of fluff in the book, I apologize in advance. That's not the goal. It is my aim to give you everything you need to be able to go out there and execute a profitable probate strategy.

In the next chapter, I'll share with you how to get ahold of the right types of probate properties to fuel your business progress, and I'll share some amazing examples of what you can do next to build your empire.

CHAPTER FOUR: HOW TO FIND YOUR CASH BUYERS

If you don't lay the right foundation, and if it's not leveled correctly, you're going to topple right over. As this book discusses real estate, I'm sure you can appreciate this analogy. So, before you move on to the content in this chapter, I can't underscore enough how critical it is for you to get those first two chapters read. More importantly, make sure you understand them before moving forward. If you haven't implemented what you've needed from the first two chapters, stop reading and go back to them. If you've already read them but haven't done what I am advising you to do, make sure you go back and take action.

If you have tackled everything you needed to do to reach this point and this chapter, awesome. Congratulations! Kudos to you on making it to this chapter. It is going to be a game-changer for you. This book was designed to enable an individual to go out and wholesale, to essentially use none of their cash, and none of their credit. I am living this reality, and I know it works.

As we go through this book together, you will learn that I like to do things in reverse. It is for this reason that we haven't gotten into how to do the probates, how to find them, and how to create the right direct mail pieces for them.

Let's not skip the line. First, it's really important that you put together a solid list of qualified cash buyers for your potential properties you'll be getting after you read this book. And, after you read this book, you're going to have an edge over your competition within your target market mainly because I'm giving you insights others haven't been taught when they were learning about how to find and flip probates.

Who Makes a Good Cash Buyer and Where the Heck Do I Find Them?

As the title of this chapter implies, you need to have the right cash buyers on your list. In my experience, this number is usually between 5-10 cash buyers that you will keep at the ready. Now, even though you have these buyers at your disposal, it takes just one person to buy the property. You're not hoping to link up people to go in on one property together at the same time. Some people say they have thousands of people on their list, and that's fine and dandy, but to do what you are trying to do, move properties, you don't need a massive list. You only need a maximum of 10 really good and qualified people. You might be thinking, *well, Jason, how would I know whether they were qualified or not? I'm a beginning flipper.* I got you. We are going to cover what you need to know to determine if a cash buyer is a good fit.

More important than knowing how to peg a viable cash buyer for your list, is that you understand what to do. I'm not talking about what we already talked about—the business steps that you need to take to make your business possible and profitable.

I'm referring to who you should contact. At this point, you have identified the key potential team players; now, it's time to contact them. Early in the game, start connecting with attorneys. Besides offering you legal advice, attorneys bring a lot of other bonuses to the table. They can refer people currently going through the process of grieving and who just inherited a property to you. If you can be that point person, you can easily ease the burden for a family going through a loss with your professionalism and efficiency. The attorneys you use will be more than happy to plug you and allow you to earn business when they know you can be trusted to take care of their clients.

Many real estate attorneys are also well-versed in investing. My attorney invests a ton in real estate and does extremely well outside of his practice. He buys properties from other wholesalers and us in the area. He's doing a ton of business, so put it on your to-dos to get involved with an attorney right away. If you have a local RIEA, a Real Estate Investors Association, connect with people there. This is a gold mine of attorneys.

If you don't have your own local Real Estate Investors Association, you can find people at meetup.com. When I began my investing business, I wish I'd had access to this kind of platform. The great thing with meetup.com is that you can find meetings for entrepreneurs, business owners, real estate investors, and marketers, as well as you can do all-around networking with other like-mind industry professionals. Most of these groups have anywhere from 25-300 people in attendance. When you have access to this many people, it opens doors, a lot of us never had 10-15 years ago.

Discover business and entrepreneur groups and connect with people at the local and national levels. I'm a big believer in networking. I love networking. And the biggest point that will work to your advantage in networking is not saying, "Hey, I'm a networker," but it has everything to do with building relationships and being authentic with the people you meet. Who you are as a person, really does matter, and has everything to do with who will want to do business with you.

Yes, these groups are great for networking. The bigger truth is they're great for getting to know people and building relationships with them. Think about it. Business is all about if people like you or not. If they don't like you, then they're not going to want to do business with you. That's an old sales adage. I know that's how it works for me. When a lot of people see me, I'm in flip flops, shorts and a T-shirt. If they don't like that and they want somebody in a suit, well that's not going to be me. I won't compromise who I am, and I encourage you to do the same.

I'm not going to dress up in a suit to try to impress somebody. If you like dressing up in a suit, that's great. I did the whole corporate America thing for a while, including the suit and tie, and it burned me out. Sure, I love wearing suits every once in a while, but who I am is a guy in shorts, a T-shirt and flip flops. So, if the people I connect with to do business don't like that, then we can both move on.

Don't forget to include in your sphere of influence, property managers as well. We've discussed this, but there is another reason why you want to seek these people out and invite them into your circle. Working with a property manager serves two advantages.

Allow me to go outside the probate conversation for a moment and ask you a question. If a property is going to be sold and you're an individual who can get that property quickly liquidated, do you think having a property manager in your sphere of influence is going to be important? With a property manager at the ready, you can be that go-to person. You could have a property manager reach out to you and say, "Hey, we've got a property that's coming up for sale. The owners want to get rid of it, and we'd love to do a deal with you." These types of connections and interactions are how business is done.

Guess how else you can find a property manager? Yep, LinkedIn. Let me just put this subject to rest and state loud and clear that you can find anyone you want, for your sphere of influence on LinkedIn. You can find the people you need on your team through social media or any of the other avenues I discussed earlier.

However, if you're not working a lot of referrals, you will have a harder time growing your business. As the saying goes (and I believe it!), "Referrals are the name of the game." A lot of people who are just starting out, have a hard time getting those referrals. That's precisely why we're going to talk about how to build those relationships and your referral pipelines. You can be one of those individuals who say when they are referencing their business, "Yeah, I built what I have on referrals." And doesn't it make sense to have as many people as possible looking out for deals for you? Referrals simply require that you take care of people who are referred to you well. Do this, and your referral network will grow as will the number of deals you close.

When you use LinkedIn, of course, understand some people are your first connections. These are the people you're already connected with. You don't want to hit these people up (for the most part) when you are seeking connections. You want to break into the second and third connections. Make sure they're in real estate. Select that industry, and then find the people within your target market.

Let's revisit the topic of real estate agents again, but this time to link to cash buyers through them. Tremendous amounts of money are moved through real estate channels. Real estate agents work with people who are selling and buying properties. Some of these agents are selling a lot of properties to individuals with cash. You want to talk to those people! Don't you think they would love to do business with you, especially if you have an off-market property? Absolutely! If we take a look right now at MLS, we're going to see that thousands of transactions have taken place over the last three to six months. Getting on board with a couple of key real estate agents who handle those transactions consistently could be an absolute game-changer for you.

When you're looking on the MLS, you can see if there's a real estate agent who's closing lots of cash transactions. They might be buying for themselves, or they might have a network of individuals who are consistently buying. Make sure you cut them in on the deal so their brokerage can be paid a commission. When you do this, you provide an incentive for them to do more deals with you. You assure them they are appreciated and that you will continue to do business with them.

Above and beyond probate, they may also send you deals because you're always finding them deals. You're making them money, and of course, this is going to make them happy. Getting to know you and establishing that relationship means you can receive other deals outside of probate. As I've stated, you're going to need two or three strategies to create the consistency you want within your business.

I hope, since you're reading this book right now, that probate will be one of those strategies. As long as you do probate the right way, you will enjoy consistency every single month. This is what you want to shoot for.

To that effect, have you considered meeting other wholesalers at your Real Estate Investors Association meetups? I mentioned using them before since they are a great resource. And they are also fairly easy to find by looking at the "we buy houses" signs you'll see on the side of the road. We'll talk about another couple of strategies for finding other wholesalers, but the "we buy houses" folks already have, more than likely, established a list of cash buyers.

Here's a fun question to consider. Do you think it would be worth it to do a JV 50/50 deal if you found the deal and the other wholesaler brought in the buyer? If there's a $20,000 spread, I'm sure you'd be fine with making $10,000 and the wholesaler making $10,000 because once you cut your teeth on your first deal together, you guys can do more and more business. That's going to help you out considerably (and it will fatten up your wallet, too). If you want to find these people, you can also go to the public recorder's office within your county and look at recently closed transactions.

Now, I will be completely honest with you; this will take a little bit of time—but keep at it, and it will pay off.

Searching for Deals and Buyers at the County Recorder's Office

If you can afford the time right now, go down to the recorder's office and check out their recently sold transactions. You can find properties without mortgage notes assigned to them and learn about people who have closed transactions with cash. People who have an established business may have to hire somebody to dig this information up. So, you could look at where you are in your beginning business in two ways. 1) If you haven't done this before and you do want to do it in the future, do the research at the recorder's office yourself, and 2) do this at least once or twice yourself so you can get it down and create a system. When you do that, somebody else can take over the digging for you.

As you will find out when you're flipping through the records, the address of the property and the mailing address are not going to be the same. Most of the time, when cash transactions are taking place, they're being bought with a business entity like an LLC. When you find that out, you can send that individual a direct mailer. Or if you want to give them a call, you can. You can also do a skip trace. If you're not familiar with that, it means you're engaging with a service to try and find that individual's information. This is a great website to use to find out this type of information: www.fastpeoplesearch.com. It's insane how accurate this website is, and you can use it absolutely for free. Consider it a slick tool to keep in your toolbox. These methodologies work to find out the people who are in charge of the property, the heirs, etc., but you can also locate this information when searching online or in person at the county recorder's office. The information you can gather in the file comprises the person's name, mailing address, and the property address for the house they just purchased. When you have this information, you can locate properties that fit the investor's buying criteria so that you won't get stuck with properties that might not sell for top dollar.

As I mentioned in the previous chapters syncing up with title companies is going to be an asset for you, especially if you can find out if they have any referrals of individuals who have done cash transactions. Now, is your brand-new title company going to cough up all that information you need ASAP? No, you have to build a relationship with them...even if you haven't closed any transactions yet. Here's a hack I learned that moved the needle for me. If you have not closed a transaction with a particular title company and you want to find out who some of the cash buyers are, use this message to get the dirt you need.

Let's just say the person's name at the title company is Joe. You will write:

"Hey, Joe. This is Jason. I just wanted to connect with you because I want to do business with you guys. I'm just getting started, and I have some off-market properties coming up, and I wanted to know if you have any investors that are looking for off-market properties at really nice discounts where they can make a substantial profit. I know you really can't give me their information, but if I were able to present a property or so to you, is there any way that you could maybe pass along that information? I've heard nothing but great things, and I would love to have a relationship with you guys where we are doing deals every month. Is there anything that we can do together?"

By posing your question like this, it puts you into a position to close some cash transactions, and when that happens, you can add the people you dealt with right into your network. Most title companies will not give away personal information. They're going to first present the information to their individual, and then it will be up to that individual if they want to reach out to you or not.

But most of the time, as long as you're getting the deals, and you're especially using the ways that I am teaching you in this book, you'll be able to partner up with whomever you want to work with.

When it comes to finding individuals you can plug into your orbit, it's also worthwhile to attend real estate auctions and even tax auctions. I like to ask my students: "Who are the people mainly attending those auctions? They're individuals with cash, right?" When you find these people that you need to put these deals to bed, they are easy to confirm because they're making the bids; they're raising their hand to make offers, and they have cash. The people you want to work with will have cashier's checks. They're ready to go and make business happen.

Attending these auctions every once in a while will definitely pay out. While you're there, give people you meet your business card or set up an appointment to have lunch. Then treat them to lunch or give them a call. If you don't have a ton of money to take people out for lunch, I completely get it. I've been there and done that. If this is your reality, it can change, but maybe hopping on a phone call or going out for a coffee might be a better option.

Our goal is to give out as much value as possible. So, how can you help these new people in your network? You need to answer this question because most people want to know how you can help them, and in return, they're going to want to help you. This is how you develop relationships with a lot of cash buyers. I'm not saying taking these actions will work out this way every time you go to these auctions but go anyway. Even if you don't have any business cards at the ready, don't let that stop you. Strive to be as prepared as you can be but take imperfect action when you need to. If you need business cards, a lot of people use Vistaprint. Between you and me, they are just okay. I grade them a five out of a 10 because they use somewhat flimsy cardstock unless you pay extra to increase the weight.

MOO is a company that also prints business cards. Their website is www.moocards.com. Get the Luxe card, and you will see a significant difference in what the card looks and feels like in your hand. Make sure to include your company logo if you have one. If you don't, that's not a big deal either. Get 50-100 cards and give those out to people who you've pegged to join your team. Don't just give out cards to anyone. I see too many people throw their cards around, and they don't value who they're giving their cards to. I don't want random strangers calling me; I want people I'm networking and building relationships with to be the ones to call.

In addition to these ways that you can use to find cash buyers, I would also recommend you check out Craigslist. Stay tuned because I will explain what you need to know regarding Craigslist in a moment.

Vetting Potential Buyers

When you are searching for the people to fill your team, make sure you practice vetting who you are recruiting. Make sure you're approaching people in the right places, whether that be at an auction or through an event at the Real Estate Investors Association, etc. It's exciting to make a new acquaintance and easy to get swept up in increasing your network. But you don't want to add someone to your list because they say to. Add quality people and practice vetting them to make sure you're not missing the mark.

Ask specific questions about what they're looking for in potential properties because you might send them 5, 10, or even 20 properties, yet they won't respond to your text if the properties aren't what they want. You want people who are going to be responsive. You can influence them to a degree by doing your homework and learning what they want. Ask questions like, what type of square footage are they're looking for? Is there a certain price or size range they need? Is there a maximum dollar amount? Finally, find out, can they purchase more than one property at one time?

Not asking those questions has a huge impact on your business. What if you have five probates? Could you sell them to just one cash buyer? Absolutely, you can. This is why you need to do your homework and find out if your buyers are willing and able to make multiple purchases. Find out their preferred location. Real estate is all about location, location, location. If it's in a D-class area, which means high crime and lots of boarded-up homes, you need to know the precise location of where they want to buy. Find out the bedroom and bath count they want. Are they mainly looking for three-bedroom, one-bath properties? There's only one way to find out this information, and that's by asking the right questions and getting detailed information. Find out if they prefer a style of property. Do they want a ranch? Do they want a two-story home? Do they want a tri-level? What kind of style home gets them motivated to buy? Some prefer ranch-style homes to convert to assisted living properties. Some buyers prefer two stories. It just depends. Again, you will never know what properties your buyer will bite on unless you ask them those questions.

The more in-depth you get with your questions; the better your buyer's list will be. If I have a list of thousands of people and I haven't asked these pointed questions, the list, in my opinion, is not useful to me. Put together a list of five to 10 solid buyers with similar criteria. You don't want to go after probates in areas that don't make sense. It will waste your time and potential marketing dollars. If your buyers are looking for similar property traits, you will have a better chance of moving your inventory. Making connections outside of social media will give you more credibility with your buyers, as well. Take the time to talk to them on the phone and get to know them. Don't waste too much time on the phone, though. And don't waste your buyer's time either. Maintain control of the conversation. Respect the fact that businesspeople like to get shit done as rapidly and smoothly as possible.

After the Vetting

After you've vetted your buyers, gathered information, and received what you've needed, then commit to sending the buyers your properties as soon as you get them. If you don't have a list yet, send them intriguing information they will care about.

Here's a method that pays off: Go to Google and type in Google Alerts. You will want to do exactly what the site advises and set up a new alert. I do this with a lot of my groups on Facebook and when we're sending out emails.

This is how setting up an alert will help you. Say, for instance, you live in Milwaukee. Then you would set up an alert for "Milwaukee real estate." When you do this, Google Alert will send you daily alerts for Milwaukee's real estate.

When you set up an alert, get ready to learn all about that market. Maybe it's a great rental market. Maybe solid deals will pop up frequently, and you can send powerful emails to your cash buyers list. When you do this and take the time to send off information and properties of value, they'll think *oh, man, Jason really knows what he's talking about. He's sending us some great information about our market we're investing in.* Do you think sending off powerful information with charts and graphs from reputable sources will be key to the business you are constructing? The answer is, "Hell, yeah!" This is especially true for some of your out-of-state individuals. They're going to get excited about seeing your name in their emails. Which gives you the attention you need to get your business off the ground.

If you don't want to use Google alerts, try www.alltop.com or www.zerohedge.com. And if you need up-to-date info on what's going on in the mortgage market or key housing index information, www.mortgagenewsdaily.com is a reliable site where you can attain insightful information for your cash buyers.

Now, you're really cooking. You're finding deals, lining up cash buyers, and conducting research to make sure your deals offer value as well as you're training up team members.

It's time to talk about email. If you don't have an email service provider already, I recommend MailChimp. MailChimp allows you to house up to 2,000 contacts for free and send out up to 12,000 emails per month...again, for absolutely nothing! You'll want to create an account and get those emails rolling because you're going to want to stay in contact with the people on your list. This is the basic marketing that you will need at this stage of the game, but you will be doing a lot more with marketing as you progress through this book.

With such an excellent plan so far, and you are sure to get a few deals under your belt.

In later chapters, we'll touch on additional sources that will allow you to implement other key systemizations for your business. Right now, you are just getting your feet wet and doing it slowly, to make sure you are using your newfound knowledge in a way that will serve you.

It's going to take a minute to find properties. So, you are right on track if that is what you are going through. In other industries, you might have heard of this time of starting out as paying your dues or cutting your teeth. In the real estate investment world, it is no different. You will get there, and every single flipper has been there too, so you're in good company. Keep at it. Send out one or two emails per week, letting your folks know about your market. Try Google Alerts or one of the other sites that I recommended to give you useful information. Even if you get a slow start, your momentum will pick up. This is why I highly recommend you use these sites.

If you don't speak with your buyers in a couple of weeks after connecting with them, reach out to them via phone or email. You could send them a text as well. If they continue to be non-responsive or late, replace them with a more reliable buyer. You have to make what you are doing a business decision, not an emotional one.

Craigslist

I skimmed over the topic of Craigslist earlier. But you should know you can also find the buyers and partners you're looking for there. On the Craigslist site, go to the area where you want to do business. If you go to the main page for your city, you'll see an area that says "services."

When you click on "services," you'll see people who you might want to get into business with. There will be a lot of posts. That's okay. Sift through the posts to try and find the people listing something similar to "we buy houses." These people could be potential JV partners; they could be cash buyers. You'll want to contact them over the phone or via text or email. When you get ahold of them, see what they're looking to do. If they're looking to JV on deals, if they're looking to buy from you, you can add those people to your list—as soon as you get confirmation over the phone, it's okay to start sending emails to them.

Other Resources

Another great website you might not think to use is called Go Section 8 at www.gosection8.com. Once at this site, find your target market by putting in your city and state and then get ready to comb through a bunch of listings. You will need to click on each listing. If you scroll down slightly on the right side, you'll see individual contact information. This allows you to contact that individual about the property.

When I make these calls, I typically say, "Hey, my name's Jason. I was contacting you about 123 Main Street. I wanted to see if it was still available." And if they say yes or no, I say the same thing, "Okay, is that property at all for sale?" Most of the time, they're going to say, "No, it's not for sale." Then I would reply, "Okay, no problem. The other reason why I was giving you a call is we're coming across off-market properties, and I wanted to see if you were in the market. We have properties that are very similar to this property I called you about that are coming in and out of our inventory quickly. Are you interested in becoming an individual we could potentially work with in the future?"

This is an effective script to use because when you find people on the Go Section 8 website, you'll see listings of properties for people who have a Section 8 voucher. This means they're getting government assistance. In addition to these people, you will also run across property managers. You can use the exact same conversation I just shared a few paragraphs back, to locate people to add to your cash buyers database.

Before you move onto the next chapter, one of the tasks I recommend you do is define a list of your cash buyers. As soon as that’s done, reach out to them with some of the information we've discussed in this chapter. Once you've done this and taken all the actions I’ve advised, you're ready for the next chapter and to massively implement and take action.

CHAPTER FIVE: FINDING AND FLIPPING PROBATES

When I talk about implementing the strategy around finding and flipping probates, a lot of folks have a tough time knowing exactly where to get the probates. Some individuals who have been doing these kinds of deals for a little while may say, "I would go down and get it at the recorder's office, who records recently filed probates." And that is true. We're going to go over this and several other strategies in this chapter that will move you a little further down the path.

Read on to discover marketing tactics you can use and a little more info on working with properties that include personal property as well as resources that you can plug and play ASAP.

All I ask for in return for sharing this information is that when you read the bonus chapter later, and you get a deal, please give us a testimonial and show us what you were able to do. If you're flipping it, to make a quick profit, show us the check. I would greatly appreciate it.

Finding Deals

There are quite a few sources you can use for finding deals, and we've talked about this previously, yet I wanted to let you in on one of the best strategies I know of. This applies when you're coming across probates or individuals who have passed away and left their properties through a trust. Working directly with attorneys has always been beneficial.

Attorneys work with probate all the time. Often the family doesn't know what they're going to do when their loved one passes, and the attorney can always give your information to them as a reference.

Here's an example.

Around mid-2008, I was just getting my feet wet with real estate after the mortgage market collapsed, and I was no longer in a job at the nation's top subprime mortgage company. Business on my own was starting to click. I really liked probate and short sales when I was first getting going, and I began to get in with some probate attorneys.

Back in the day, I would Google attorneys who dealt with wills and helped people set up their retirements with trusts, etc. This type of attorney fits my needs, and I would send off message after message via email. I would only use email at first because I didn't want to give them a call out of the blue without them at least knowing who I was. So, I would always send an email first, and then I would get them on the phone.

A few attorneys did reach back out to me. I took some out to lunch. In doing so, I learned, you might want to rethink this idea. I quickly realized attorneys like to go to nice restaurants, which are typically expensive. I didn't have as much money when I was first starting as I'd just gotten married and was expecting my first child. Hindsight is 20/20!

So if you don't have a huge budget, I would highly encourage you not to take them out. Have a phone call with them or maybe go to their office instead. You could also go out for coffee, as I mentioned. I personally don't drink coffee, yet I'll still take people out to places that have coffee. This is a much more affordable way to connect in person.

My primary mission was to meet an attorney whose focus was wills, trusts, and setting up protective legal measures for a family in case something were to happen. Well, lo and behold, an attorney gave me a shot. He was doing a ton of work with family members and came across a family who had come to his office needing help. They were in a trust. Their mother had recently passed away and left them the house. An executor had been assigned.

One of the family members was out of the country, and another lived in California. The property was in Indiana. Both family members wanted to get rid of the property and all of the belongings as quickly as possible because they were completely distraught. They were sad. They were mourning, and they didn't want to continue feeling the agony from losing their loved one.

We'll talk about handling personal property in just a moment. Because I want you to know there are huge opportunities that will allow you to make an additional profit while also satisfying the individuals you're going to be working with.

In this deal, we were able to agree on terms. Since we were dealing with a trust, the contract didn't have to go through probate, and it closed. The attorney was extremely happy because the clients were extremely happy. I closed when I said I was going to close, and this meant a great deal to all the parties.

The reason I closed is that I had cash buyers. It's critical that you have cash buyers, especially when you're going to be working in this business. It wasn't hard for me to get those cash buyers lined up either. I probably only had five to eight of them in 2008, and my list has grown over time.

Working with attorneys gives you such an advantage.

I would highly recommend you connect with them and let them know you are available.

When I sent off the email to the attorneys in my target, my message was pretty short and sweet. Let's say the attorney's name is Joe. I would say, "Hi Joe, my name is Jason. I'm a real estate investor here in Indianapolis. I wanted to reach out to you as we're working closely with individuals who have lost loved ones, and they're looking to liquidate the property they've inherited. Please reach back out to me if you have any clients that are interested in liquidating the property and receiving a fast and fair cash offer. My phone number is (insert number). Thanks, Jason."

Now, if they didn't email me back or I didn't hear from them, I would give them a call. A lot of attorneys are super busy, they're either with clients, in litigation, or doing trial work, etc. So I would give them a call and say the same thing I said in the email, only this time, over the phone. "Hi Joe, my name's Jason. I sent you an email the other day and wanted to reach back out to you, in reference to seeing if we could do business together and if any of your clients might be interested in receiving a fast and fair offer on a property they may have just inherited from a loved one who passed away. We can make this process extremely seamless, and they don't have to worry about taking care of the property or anything like that. Is there any way we can meet up for a cup of coffee?

In my case, as I told you before, unfortunately, I would meet up and take them out for very expensive lunches...not just coffee!

Seriously, just do the coffee route!

Open an Old-School Newspaper

Emailing and calling is one way to reach an attorney. Now, we're going to talk about the other route, which is, finding them in newspapers or through conducting online searches—and we'll dive deeper into that method in a second.

In case you think the newspaper is a dinosaur, it's not. Under legal notices, look for probate or deaths—not the obituaries. This is a huge section, and because states often require what's called a notice of creditors to be printed in a newspaper or in general circulation, you can find the people you are looking for there.

Subscribe to these papers in your target market and check them daily. When you do this, you can find the information and notice of deaths. These notices are printed daily mainly to satisfy the debt collectors. They are part of the probate process and state simply that a person passed away, and they're trying to pay off any debts which could be out there.

Most of the time, when probate is going on, especially if the executor is in line, those debts are going to be paid off. The notice in the paper fulfills the criteria to have the information out in public circulation.

Head to the County Assessor's Office

A county assessor's office usually requires a name or case number to get the info you need. A case number can be found on the notice, and you can get the name of the people you need from the notice of death that's in the ad or online. Every single county in the country is going to require different information and have different rules for entering the information. You may have to go down to the county or research online as to what the rules are for your location.

Use Your Title Company

All title companies operate differently. In attorney-closed states, the process will be quite different from non-attorney-closed states. Title companies and attorneys can find out information from a QCD or quitclaim deed. When somebody passes away, the quitclaim deed must be in place to purchase the property.

Let's assume a mother passes away, and the son inherits the property as the executor of the state. A quitclaim deed will more than likely be in process. Now, sometimes the executor can sign over the title depending on what the title company is going to do and depending on how long the executor of the estate is going to have this particular property. Typically, this is done if the property is going to be held for a certain period, and the title company is aware of recently filed quitclaim deeds. You can find out this information relatively quickly.

Subscribing to Lists

Yet another way to find probates is through a mail house or by subscribing to certain lists. One of the sites we recommend is Yellow Letters Complete—website: www.yellowletterscomplete.com. I know the owner very well. We do a lot of direct mail pieces and postcards through them. The individuals at Yellow Letters Complete can do all of this for you, so you don't have to handwrite the letters. These are great, high-response marketing pieces that we'll go over later in the chapter.

If you want to try and purchase a list, just know some states are nondisclosure states, and you will not be able to access or pull particular data—Indiana is a nondisclosure state, for example. A source I recommend is ListSource—website: www.listsource.com. In using these lists, you can also find cash buyers for specific transactions. If you want a step-by-step video tutorial, visit my YouTube channel. Once on YouTube, just type into the search engine box "Jason Lucchesi," and you'll see all the YouTube videos I've added that explain exactly how ListSource works. Then you can duplicate in your business what we are doing very easily without any delays.

Good Ol' Google

Using the notice of death can help you find a lot of probates, especially if you want to get information from the public recorder's office. Simply go to Google and search "notice of death" and then "your area." For example, "notice of death Indianapolis."

When you do this search, you can find individuals who have recently passed away. The search will provide their name, the area where they lived, and the age at their time of passing. In some cases, it may note surviving family members. Getting the name leads to learning a lot more information. Knowing the area where they lived, and the descendants' names are crucial. You need that information to make that initial connection.

With this basic information, we can now use the internet to get everything else we need. And the best part? This search was free. Now, as I've recommended in the past, if you wanted to do a skip trace to find certain individuals, you can do so by using a free website called Fast People Search—website: www.fastpeoplesearch.com.

Once you have accessed the death notices, record the descendants listed.

Understand, when you use this method of searching that notices are posted on a daily or weekly basis. It depends on your area. Check them out in the locations where you'll be investing in, and make sure you come back and do another search when the new notices will be published.

I mentioned setting up Google Alerts earlier, and I want to bring it up again because it is that important and useful. The Google alert I would encourage you to activate is "notice of death" and then "your area"—as we discussed. Set up that Google alert so every time the notices are refreshed, the information will automatically be sent to your inbox. I recommend you have a Gmail account to send the notices to, so you don't experience any hiccups since Gmail will talk to Google Alerts nicely. Do this, and your email will give you

multiple deals and everything you need to contact the right people and get the ball rolling.

Info You Need to Put Together Your Offer FAST

Now, we're going to cover a lot concerning the due diligence period of being able to do offers and what to look for in later content. If you want to put together offers very quickly, it's crucial you use a maximum allowable offer, or your MAO, that will calculate what you should be offering. Depending on your market, you're going to want to offer anywhere between 65% to 80% of ARV, or After Repaired Value.

Again we will cover the information concerning repairs and comps within the due diligence chapter of this book, but we need to touch on it now, so you know exactly how to do a property valuation immediately. The main reason why we recommend 65% to 80% of the ARV is that every market is different.

For instance, Indiana is going to be relatively lower in ARV than Arizona. The ARV all depends on the competitiveness of your market and how saturated it is. As of right now, deals are not readily available. Most of the available inventory is going to be found using the probate method discussed in this book, and through what I call sub-markets. The sub-markets are on the edge of the larger metropolitan area and are not as competitive. They offer you the opportunity to lock up deals at discounted prices without you having to fight tooth and nail. Keep in mind the buyers you have for the larger areas may not be interested in the small sub-markets. You may have to get buyers interested in the areas that present you with the most opportunity. So if you do get a property, especially in a larger metropolitan area, it could be 75% to 80% ARV because you're dealing with an executor who knows the market and where it's difficult to liquidate properties quickly. This could potentially pose a problem. So knowing your numbers and knowing what properties are selling for is extremely valuable in this particular scenario.

Marketing

In the following paragraphs, I'll explain the exact steps you'll need to take for your marketing campaign to be a success. I am only touching slightly on some aspects of creating offers because you need an overview to understand this chapter's content. When you combine this preliminary information with the marketing information I am sharing below; you will find success as a real estate investor.

In this chapter, we're covering finding and getting deals under contract and being able to flip them. This book is designed for the wholesaler. Now, if you are a rehabber or you like to buy properties and hold them, you can take advantage of the strategies we have discussed so far in this book and my other books: *Right Flipping Now*—to help you locate deals outside of probate, and *Find the Flipping Deals*—which gives you the deepest dive into flipping properties.

Note that the number of steps of each of these numbers corresponds with a week number. Step 1 happens during week one and so forth.

A Method to the Marketing Madness

Step 1

Now, let's talk about the marketing you will need to do as part of your business. You will want to utilize a direct mail piece. But let me correct a misunderstanding. You're not going to be sending out thousands of pieces unless you're doing a couple of states at a time and several counties within those states. When you use direct mail, you're going to want to do drip campaigns—which enable you to continue those high touches with your client. Did you know most people don't want to do business with somebody they haven't at least had a conversation with or experienced at least five and six touch touchpoints?

Drip campaigns are meant to last between five to six weeks. After that, the emails or drips slow down to monthly contacts for a year. That's why I told you about the drip campaigns you can create from Yellow Letters and or postcards—do whatever works within your budget to reach the most people who will want to work with you.

Note, since you are using some automated services, make sure to be sensitive to whomever you address the letter to.

When People Lose a Loved One

Keep a couple of things in mind when dealing with folks who've just lost a loved one.

The topic can be quite sensitive, and people don't mean to be rude when talking to you, but sometimes this can happen. This is why it's important to have a thick skin.

Practice creating that thick skin every day, and don't let it hurt your feelings or take what people have to say personally. In many instances, people are trying to figure out how to deal with everything that happened. Losing a loved one is extremely, extremely tough, and folks do get upset. So don't let it get to you.

Not everyone will be ready to talk about the property, especially if the loss *just* happened. So, take good notes about what you discussed, how you discussed it, and anything that might be of use to you in the next follow-up. When you do this, you are a shoo-in, and the person will be more likely you remember you. Be sure to set a follow-up call with anyone who isn't ready to talk about the property.

I would normally say, "Would it be okay if I follow-up with you in two weeks?" If they say, "No. That's okay;" I would then say, "Would it be okay if I follow-up, and see how everything's going with you in the next 30 days?" That question is typically a good measure of if they are okay with me calling back. If they are, this is a good sign. They will more than likely entertain an offer down the road. Maybe they haven't quite reached a decision yet. Maybe they're the executor, and they need to talk to two or three other descendants about the property.

If they are receptive to your asking to follow-up, make sure you give them a good contact number to call you back. And if you do want to set up a number, so they don't have your direct cell phone number, you can use a forwarding number. Google Voice works well. I'm recommending a lot of Google items because they're easy to use, and if you have team members, you can share Google docs, too.

Step 2 — Call

If you're unable to send direct mail, that's completely fine. Please complete the next recommendation—phone calls.

If you can't make phone calls during the day, you might find success by freeing up time in your day with a method called time blocking. Regardless of if you are a full-time or part-time worker, you need to be time blocking. Part-time people might work from 9:00 AM to 5:00 PM and then get home to do dinner and stuff with the kids or maybe go to the gym. I hate to say it, but that doesn't matter. You still need to prioritize your time, so you're working on your business and then getting back to your other responsibilities as quickly as possible.

Now, I can't place any guarantees on how quickly you'll be able to leave your job, but I do recommend you implement time blocking. If you're sleeping eight to nine hours a night, try sleeping less, so you have time to work your business. Once you start getting some deals closed, you can enjoy the fruits of your labor. A lot of people don't put in the work that's needed to get to the success level they are aiming for. You can make this business work as long as you're devoting a quality 5-10 hours per week to it. If you do that, you will see the results.

Obviously, the more quality time you can devote, the more results you will see. I recommend you check from state to state to see if you can do what's called a ringless voicemail, also known in the community as an RVM. We like to use Slybroadcast—website: www.slybroadcast.com. When you use a ringless voicemail, your call goes right to the recipient's inbox as a voicemail. When they receive it, they will either give you a callback or not.

Before you do this, make sure you update your list and remove everyone you have made contact with from step one—week one. All we're doing with the ringless voicemail is leaving a message similar to this, "Hi, my name is Jason. I was just giving you a call about your property at 123 Main Street. Please give me a call back at (phone number). Talk to you soon."

Or you can use this message, which is very general: "Hi, my name is Jason. I was giving you a call about your property that you recently inherited. Please give me a call back. My number is (insert number). Thanks for your time." That's very short, sweet, and right to the point. This second script does generally receive a higher number of responses back since it's a little more forthcoming.

It's so easy. Just create a simple message like the ones recommended and send them to your updated list. Regard the inbound calls the same way you do the mailer. Some people may not be ready to talk about the property. Still, be prepared to take notes and schedule that follow-up call as needed.

Even though you are leaving a ringless voicemail, I want you to be prepared to take the phone calls that come back in. Don't let them go to *your* voicemail. This is the main reason I suggest you use an answering service like Hosted Numbers. You really shouldn't have any calls go to voicemail. When you have a hot caller or deal, you need to be reachable to help the person in need while helping yourself.

Step 3

We're onto step three, aka week three, which entails the handling of the postcard. We're using a smaller postcard because the size allows us to cut costs. Before you send any off, update your list. That means everybody you've talked to from week one and two are off of the list. They're not receiving this postcard.

The postcard is going to be very similar to the letter. You will address the person by their first name on it, like this: "Dear Bill, I offer my deepest sympathies during a time that is nothing short of trying. Many people find the challenge of selling their loved one's estate difficult, and I may be able to help. I can offer a quick cash purchase of your property at 123 Main Street in an as-is condition for fair market value, which could help you to resolve other obligations. Please call me at 555-555-5555 with any questions. Thanks, Jason."

We're not coming across as being pushy or pitchy or anything like that in this postcard. We're trying to offer help during a difficult time. Make sure the return calls back from these postcards are either answered by you, or by the service noted above because otherwise, it's a lost opportunity. If you do hear back from somebody and they're not ready to talk, do what I've advised and set up a follow-up call as necessary.

Step 4 - Text message

Step four and week four is the text message. You might have noticed we're making multiple efforts to reach people and get in front of them. We want to let people know we are interested.

I recommend a couple of different websites that you can use to send your text messages. Call Loop and RingCentral are some of the big ones. Hosted Numbers—website: www.hostednumbers.com can be used both as an answering service and for text messaging.

Before you send the text message, update your list. Remove everybody from weeks one through three. You're going to want to use a text messaging service unless you want to text each individual manually from your phone or use Google Voice to do texting.

Use a simple message to get them to call you back, like this "Hey, I just wanted to see if you got my message about the house. Call me back." Then leave your number and first name. Again, texting is short, as we've tried to do with all of our messages. We do this to pique their curiosity and not drown them in information they don't need. If they haven't been reaching back at this point, a text is a simple way to allow them to get back to you, and it makes contacting you a snap. Smartphones these days, allow a person to simply touch the recipient's info a couple of times to make the call back.

Still, recognize and accept you won't hear back from some people. These people either are not getting your earlier messages, or they might be ignoring them. Maybe they have a lot going on and are not sure what they are doing about the property. If you have contacted them via the steps noted in this chapter, they have your information and can contact you when they are ready.

Now we're ready to talk about the final steps.

At this point, you have made four contact attempts, meaning the remaining leads are no good, or the person is not ready to talk to you since they have not been in touch with you despite your multiple attempts to talk.

Of course, you don't want to be stuck with only these duds. You should be getting new leads as you conduct business and make contact with potential clients. Keep that pipeline full!

When you have followed up multiple times, but the person still hasn't responded, add them, and others who fit those criteria into a final follow-up list. We don't want to spend too much of the marketing budget on stale leads. Yet we still want to grab whatever deals are left in this list before dropping them.

Step 5

Step five could be another postcard. This time, you're sending a simple postcard with a more urgent message.

If you still don't hear back, we will take one more stab at it.

Step 6

If, after five weeks, you aren't getting the results you want, it's time for one last-ditch effort. Send the final effort to communicate: the ringless voicemail "RVM." Let me state that I highly doubt absolutely nobody will call you based on the marketing you'll be doing, but just in case, you can send off an RVM. When I send these, I say something to the effect of, "Hi, this is Jason. I'm calling about your property one last time. If you're looking to receive a cash offer based off the fair market value of the home, give me a call at 555-555-5555. Talk soon!" Again, as is the case with the second postcard, this message is more urgent; you will let the person know this will be the last time you will contact them.

If you have received any type of a follow-up or a call, saying they weren't interested, move them to your monthly follow-up.

When we do this, we force them to tell us to leave them alone. If they don't tell you to go away, they might want to do business with you. It will be one or the other. More than likely, they're not going to keep stringing you along.

Either they're going to flip you the bird through the phone, or they're going to want to do business with you. You have to have a great follow-up system if you want to be a successful investor. To do this, use Google Calendar or whatever type of calendar you want to use, so you know when to follow-up with folks. The beauty of it is you can set up as many follow-ups as you want within those calendar applications.

Every Kind of Sale

As you progress your leads into closes, you will be dealing with all kinds of sales. Here's the list so you can familiarize yourself:

- Private sale. The attorney usually handles a private sale, and bids are solicited independently. The attorney will invite bidders to submit their bids in sealed envelopes, and the highest bid is accepted.
- Public auction. Similar to the private sale, this auction is usually held at an attorney's office in a traditional auction fashion. Again, the highest bid wins.
- Direct from the heirs. This happens when the property has had little to no exposure to the market. You could speak with the executor to get it started.

We've never had to deal with a private sale or a public auction. Because we've set up the marketing funnel and had attorneys on standby as well as title companies to work with directly, we can bypass the private sale and public auction. We can go directly to the heirs, which is the best opportunity for you to get the property at the lowest possible price. I consider this a win-win situation.

Personal Property

Personal property is all the property within the estate at the time of death. In many cases, families don't want the hassle of trying to clean out a house while mourning their loved one. They will sell the property as-is with everything inside. Sometimes, this can be a treasure trove of hidden gems you can sell-off. Handling the private property makes for a smooth transaction for the family and eliminates their need to worry or fight about possessions.

In one of our deals, a car was included with the property. This was an early 2000s Honda with very low miles. It was the mom's car for getting from point A to point B and was well maintained. It came with records noting oil changes, tune-ups, tire rotations, and every other preventative maintenance record. Mom made sure she kept up with the car. It was in great condition; the tires and brakes were good; everything was a dream.

Once we got to the house, we took the car to CarMax. If you aren't familiar with CarMax, they will give you a check for the car, whether you buy a car from them or not. We got close to $15,000 in cash on top of the profit made on the property, which was near $20,000. So between the car and wholesaling the property, we netted nearly $35,000 in profit. And this all came about because the executors wanted to get rid of the property as quickly as possible.

Marketing Info

I've set up a specific webpage where you can download all the marketing pieces reviewed in this chapter. All you need to do is go to www.noflippingexcuses.com/marketing-pieces. Enter your first and last name, so we know you're a real person, and you will get an immediate email sent to you with downloads of the marketing pieces we use, accompanied by the scripts we use when talking to the actual executors of these properties. With these tools in hand, you will know what to say to executors and heirs word for word.

I recorded an actual phone call I was on, transcribed it, and am sharing it with you. I'm not huge on using scripts, but I do think they can be handy, especially if you don't know exactly what to say. However, they can also sound a little too rehearsed. What I'm sharing with you is not a call from 10 or 15 years ago, either. All the strategies and tactics that will be at your disposal are being used right now by us in today's market.

A Big Fat Bonus

Have you heard of list stacking? I want to make sure you're successful in executing the steps in this book, and list stacking will help you out big time as it decreases your marketing budget significantly. List stacking means you are going to select the people from your mailing list who seem like they are more motivated to work with you. So you will filter your lists in this way and target some of your campaigns to them. Remember, one of the only ways to find motivated homeowners who may want to sell their property is by becoming a problem-solver. Do you think someone who just inherited a property who lives out-of-state might be motivated to sell if they owe $4,500 in property taxes, have a foreclosure judgment for $40,000, and a code violation for $1,500 compared to someone who just has a vacant house?? I'd think the person with multiple problems who needs someone to be a problem-solver can come in to help out immediately compared to the non-stacked list. This is a pretty significant difference when looking at who to send out direct mail to.

Remember that the probate strategy by itself is already is pretty niched down, meaning you're not typically chasing after 20,000 vacant house leads. I'd never mail off to a list that size with that many homeowners, and here's why. I personally know folks who send to such a massive audience weekly and/or monthly, and it's a complete waste. They might get 2-4 deals but to get those few, they spend a lot of money on advertising.

Our company does list stacking on every direct mail campaign we fire off. The stacking of multiple lists adds layers of motivation levels for your homeowners that a lot of your competitors fail to take advantage of. Most folks do a full blow "Billy Kung-Fu" with direct mail and don't look at the important details that might appeal to homeowners. We want to give these homeowners more than one reason to give us a call.

We focus on four filters in our criteria before firing off a campaign to a list:

- Value of the home
- Code violation (below are what we look for)
    - Housing and property (tall grass, overgrown vegetation, etc.)
    - Garbage and rubbish disposal (signs of vacancy)
    - Vacancy notification (abandoned home)
- Delinquent property taxes
- Pre-foreclosure

When you stack some of your lists (don't do them all or you may not have a list to mail to!), you can, for example, take a list of 5,000 homeowners and narrow it down to 200. Doing this saves you a ton of money and, in most cases, gives you a 30-40% response rate from happy homeowners. The average response rate from other investors who blow money on 5,000+ mail pieces with one filter (the house being vacant) is a whopping 1-2%—that's if you're a decent marketer. Save your marketing dollars and invest wisely. Just remember when everyone zags you should zig. Don't follow the herd as it may not lead you to where you want to be in your business. I do hope you enjoyed this extra bonus piece and plan on using it in your campaigns.

In the upcoming chapters, we will be talking about due diligence and exit strategies. You don't want to miss the mind-blowing bonus chapter either, which offers you all the insider tips I have on loading up your potential properties list.

Before you turn the page, double-check the information you have learned here. Review the notes you've taken; dot all your I's and cross all your T's. Make sure you are moving in the right direction, and at the pace you desire. Remember, this isn't a race; it's a marathon. You don't have to sprint unless you want to. Whether you're a pacer or a racer, we'll see you in the next chapter!

CHAPTER SIX: DOING DUE DILIGENCE

A lot of investors, especially brand-new investors just getting into the business, tend to overlook doing their due diligence. They get excited and feel like they have a deal, and that's enough. They might think *we're going to make money, just like we see on the television shows.* But those shows do a disserve to people because they imply you can make big money quite easily. That's true in some cases, but what's also true is that you do have to do your due diligence to figure out if you have a deal worth working.

In this chapter, we're going cover due diligence because it is one of the most overlooked aspects of real estate investing. It doesn't matter if you're wholesaling, rehabbing, or doing buy and hold properties. We need to cover this topic before we move on to exit strategies in the next chapter and the exclusive bonus information in the final chapter. As I mentioned before, this bonus information is shared with only those people who attend our high-end coaching events. We charge more because most people make back five to 10 times the amount of their initial investment. I am giving you this information because this book is all about giving you everything you need to go out, find probate deals, and help people out. It's not all about making money. It's about helping other people. When you do this, you will make the profits you desire for your business and lead the life you want.

That said, make sure if you need to go over this chapter multiple times that you do so. I'm going to start by talking about what's called a comparative market analysis, and this is the first action you need to take when executing your due diligence. You will need this information for crafting and creating your maximum allowable offer (MAO) that we're going to present to the person who wants to sell their property. In this case, it's going to be a homeowner who just went through a death in the family. They're the executor of the estate. They've got heirs and descendants, and they're trying to make a decision as quickly as possible.

Better To Be Safe Than Sorry

It's so important to make sure that the areas you're looking to do business in aren't in high crime areas. I don't see a lot of investors jumping up for joy when you tell them you have an amazing property in a "D" class neighborhood. Most investors run for the hills when you bring up a certain area. You know the areas I'm talking about. These are the areas where your navigation system has you go a "short" route which takes you through a neighborhood making you think nervously inside; *oh shoot, please don't make me stop at a red light!* Then you're yelling at the kids in a scared but stern voice, "Roll up the windows now!" The car doors are locked, and the music turned off. Your eyes are popping out, and all of sudden, you can see in 360-degree rotation. You know the neighborhoods I'm talking about.

These are the classifications of neighborhoods:

- A-Class: Upper class, gated communities, private schools nearby, high employment, new construction for homes and businesses, etc.
- B-Class: Mid to upper-middle class, great communities, great employment, highly rated

public schools, new construction, some rental/Airbnb properties, etc.

- C-Class: Low to mid-middle class, low crime, high amount of rental with a mixture of Airbnb properties, new construction, middle rate public schools, good employment, etc.
- D-Class: Low income, low rated schools, high crime, boarded-up homes, not a lot of job opportunities, older homes that need a lot of work, high foreclosures, etc.

The best way to find out if an area you're going to start wholesaling properties in is located in a safe place is to first have a list of cash buyers/investors who'll be purchasing properties from you. They will tell you where they'd like to buy. It's crucial that you find out where these investors are buying, so you know the areas to avoid like the plague. An instant way to make one of your cash buyers go "bye-bye" on you is to send them a property that is completely opposite from what they told you they were looking for.

The second-best way to find out about the areas you are interested in is by using websites like www.spotcrime.com, www.crimereports.com, and the National Sex Offender Public Website www.nsopw.gov. You can easily spot problem areas based on a variety of rankings and resources: forms of burglaries, vandalism, street views on Google to see boarded-up homes, low rated schools, etc. You can also ask a local real estate agent for investors' contact information so they can tell you which areas to stay away from. I wanted to make sure I included this information, so you don't waste precious time with your process of trying to make sure a deal is really a deal. There is nothing more important than your time. Don't waste it on deals that'll never make it to the finish line.

Running Comps

If you have access to the MLS, run the numbers to do a comparative analysis or comps. You need to do this before you get the property under contract. Because while this is the first thing you will do with a new deal, the last thing you want to do is make an offer on a property to get a property under contract without knowing your numbers. It's a waste of time for you, and it could ruin the relationship with your owner of record—now the executor of the estate. How can you even begin to put together a price if you have no idea what a reasonable price is?

Now, let's talk about what to do when you're creating a comparative market analysis, aka a CMA. You don't want to go any further than six months back unless you live in a rural area of the country, or the properties are three to five-acre lots. In cases like these, you're going to have to go a little bit further out. You might have to go back nine months, 12 months, and maybe even 18 months, depending on your location.

Next, pull at least three to four properties similar to the subject property. Let's say, for example, we've got a two-story property with a fully finished basement. We should only be looking at properties like that. If we have a three-bedroom, one and a half bath, we shouldn't be looking at four-bedroom, two-bath homes. Unless you're an appraiser and you know how to deduct and add for certain features of a home, you shouldn't be using those criteria. Now, you could use an agent if you're willing to pay what's called a

BPO (Broker Price Opinion), which will cost you anywhere between $50 to $75. Are they worth it? Yes, especially if it's within your budget. If you don't have this in your budget, then don't do it.

These three to four properties allow you to properly justify your price, which will be a negotiations standpoint for when you're figuring out your maximum allowable offer. If your maximum allowable offer doesn't come to the number that the owner, aka the executor of the estate, is presenting to you, then you can present evidence of what properties are selling for within the area.

I also recommend you don't go further than a one-mile radius from the subject property. For example, here in Indianapolis, if you go south, you could literally see houses worth $150,000 on one street, or go one street or area over, and all of a sudden, they are $30,000, or $40,000. It's extremely important that you know your area. If you don't know the area, you need a realtor on your team. We've talked about your sphere of influence; this is where having the resource of a realtor is critical for you to move forward. One final tip for pulling comps is to use Google Maps. This will allow you to see things about the property and can give you satellite and street views, etc.

We hardly ever visit the properties. But if you're just getting started in the business, I do recommend you start looking at the properties, to get a good feel for what's potentially needed. Do the floors or carpet need to be replaced? Does it need new paint or new roofing? If you're not handy, like me, it is important to get a good feel for what could potentially be needed, especially if you're going to walk the property with the contractor—which we'll get to later on in this chapter when we also cover working with bids.

For argument's sake, let's say you don't have access to the MLS. I'm not a licensed real estate professional, I'm not an agent and never have been, but I also don't need to be. You can use Zillow for finding sold comps within the area. Type in the address of the property, and then Zillow will give you a selection of what you want to be shown. Take off all the active listings, and anything that's potentially coming up. All you want to do is click on "sold." When you do this, you will see the sold properties. Then you can take it a step further and make a radius of the property. The color-coding of the dots on Zillow for this function will be yellow. These dots will tell you the prices properties have sold for, and you can find the sold dates as well.

This is a great way to see what properties you need to pay attention to and include in your assessment, especially if you don't have MLS access. You can use this information to easily put together your three comps to create an actual ARV. Here's an example of a scenario you might come across. Let's say we have a property at $205,000 that we're going to use as a comp. It's a perfect property for what we're looking for. Then we have another property that is at $202,500. The third comp is $198,500.

We will take all three of those numbers, which add up to $606,000 and divide that by three, giving us $202,000 for an after-repair value (ARV).

Now, let's roll in another consideration. The property we're going to be purchasing is selling for as much as it has been updated. Meaning kitchens are going to be completely updated to the current year. Not from the 70s or 60s or even 50s. The carpet will be updated. We're slapping on a fresh coat of paint. The bathrooms will be done. The house will look new because we will have completely revamped it from a 50s look to the current trends. Properties sell quickly when they have brand new kitchens and bathrooms; they sell quickly when they have a nice open floor plan.

It's important when we're using comparable property sales that they're pretty accurate to our subject property that we're performing the maximum allowable offer on. If our house is a ranch, we shouldn't compare it to a bi-level because those are two totally different styles of home. It's important to be close to the bedroom and bathroom count along with the square footage. Depending on where you live, the amount of garage space could play a pretty big role. You've got to think about the fact, that for instance, the home you're putting under contract has been the same since 1973 without any updates. Old interiors lead to a lot of updates in the kitchen and with the flooring, painting, electrical wiring, plumbing, roof, bathrooms, windows, HVAC, and possibly more. All of these repairs will have to be accounted for in the MAO you perform. That's why I've included sites you can use to help determine costs so you will have accurate numbers. This accurate number can be used when making the initial offer to purchase from the executor.

As wholesalers, we need to envision when we walk into these homes, what a rehabber wants to do to the property. We're not always going to be synced up with what our end buyer wants to do. But it is smart to get an idea of what the likely repairs might be. If our main goal is to wholesale properties to investors who want to purchase as a fix n' flipper, it's a great idea to put ourselves in their shoes. A lot of wholesalers fail to put together rehab costs in their MAO figure, and this tends to bite them in the rump when it comes time to flip the deal. If a lot of work needs to be done on the property, but you haven't accounted for that, you'll more than likely have a purchase and sales agreement with an accepted offer at a price you can't do anything about because you didn't add in $30,000 in repair costs. If this happens, an egg is on your face, and you'll have to back out of the deal, potentially losing your earnest money deposit. Trust me, when it comes to handyman work, I'm completely useless, so coming up with a rehab budget is tough for me. At the same time, I also understand how important it is to identify what's needed in the house. I'd recommend you always think about the main selling points of a house. What do you note about the landscaping when you pull up? What do you see when you first enter the home and as you walk through it (nice flooring, lighting, neutral colors, bathrooms, bedroom sizes, and, most importantly, the kitchen?).

After we've done our CMA, we need to calculate our maximum allowable offer. Most people get this number wrong. Within this chapter, I'm giving you the knowledge and tools to craft offers that you can feel comfortable putting out there.

Calculating the MAO

To assess our maximum allowable offer (MAO), we need to figure our profit. In other words, how much money do you want to make on this deal? Is it going to be $15,000, $20,000, $30,000? You need to include this number because that's going to be a factor, and we're going to be discussing this momentarily.

Next, you need to know the rehab budget. I know we're not doing rehabs, but if you are going to be doing the rehab yourself, you need to include the rehab cost. And we are going to do this every time we are calculating this amount, regardless of if we're wholesaling, rehabbing, or doing a buy and hold. Include that number so you will get the full profit that you want to make. Now, one of the ways we can estimate a rehab budget is to use a contractor. We're not going rogue and charging into this deal with no contracting experience, or no experience remodeling a home, just eyeballing the property. That's not the way to do it, and you will be ill-prepared for the reality of what the actual numbers will be if this is how you figure your MOA.

If you don't have a contractor, no worries! You can find contractors all over the place. One area I recommend you check out is a site is called Thumbtack—website: www.thumbtack.com. Another website is called Blue Hammer—website: www.bluehammer.com. Both of those websites are extremely easy for you to use. You can also use Angie's List. Find a contractor with good reviews and have them come out so you can explain what you want to do. Then see if you can get a quote or maybe a general idea of how much it's going to cost to rehab the property.

If they are going to do a bid or a quote, sometimes this costs $50 to $100. What you are willing and wanting to pay depends on your marketing budget. It also depends on if you can get this deal at a discount and flip it quickly to an end buyer who will have the property sold quick. You want to make really great connections and relationships with people so they will constantly come to you for more deals in the future. This is another reason it is important that you come up with a proper rehab budget. You need to be professional and know your numbers and what the hell you are talking about. Use one of the three recommended sites to come up with a proper rehab budget.

The property must be insured. As a wholesaler, and in using an assignment of the contract, you won't become the owner of record or appear on the chain of title. And since you're not going to own the property, you don't need to have insurance. Your ultimate end buyer will carry the insurance, the type of which will depend on what the end buyer does with the property. We always like to add the insurance into our maximum allowable offer, to ensure we've included all of our numbers into how much potential profit can be earned when the transaction is closed. Keep in mind that your MAO figures are always for you and your team, and not the end buyer who is going to close on the property. They can do their own numbers. As long as we give the property to them for a steal, they'll never question our asking price. Call up your insurance agent to get a quote on how much it would cost to have the property insured while it's under construction. You don't want to say it's vacant. Clarify with your agent that this is going to be a property under construction, so your agent can give you the lowest possible insurance premium on the property.

Next, we have to figure in property taxes. When we're buying the property, the properties are always going to be paid in arrears. They will be paid by the individual/seller/executor of the estate. But remember, your ultimate end buyer is reselling the property, they're going to have to pay for taxes in arrears. Add in those figures when you are estimating how much property taxes are going to be.

Don’t forget utilities. You need a general estimate of what the utilities will be. Shoot for what utilities are going for within the area. If the executor of the estate is still maintaining the property, you can ask what the utilities are, and they'll be more than happy to share this information with you. Utilities are going to play a factor when you put together your maximum allowable offer.

Include your title company closing cost. This cost comprises every cost needed to record documentation, procure title insurance premiums, and everything else that needs to be done to ensure the property can smoothly shift from the owner of record, or the executor of the estate to your ultimate end buyer—especially, if you're going to be doing what's called an assignment of contract—which is discussed in-depth in the exit strategy chapter. If you are going to be using a transactional funder—which is covered in the next chapter, make sure to plug in this number too, so you can see how it affects the deal.

The Exception to Wholesaling

If you don’t do a wholesale transaction, and you have to keep the property for a couple of weeks before your end buyer purchases it from you, you can secure a private money lender who can bridge the gap for you. You might strike a deal with them where they say, "I'll lend you the money for the two weeks, but you're going to have to pay X, Y, Z." You guessed it that X, Y, Z is going to have to be placed into your expenses, too. We are this careful with our numbers because we don’t want to jack around with our profit. That's how we get paid! That's how we make money! So, get precise. If you are looking at flipping and probate as a business and not a hobby, then you need to take these numbers seriously. If you want to make six or seven figures a year, these numbers need to be spot on.

When it comes to expenses such a property taxes, insurance, and utilities, I always like to round up, so my figures are a little bit higher than what I'm quoting. When I do this, I won't be surprised at closing. I suggest you do the same. If, for instance, normal title company closing costs are $1,500. I'll double-check that figure, and then to be sure I'm covered, add in $1,800. It's always nice at closing when you receive a little bit more in profit because you padded the deal. It's exciting and fun.

MAO Example

Let's cover an example together, so you have an idea of how to put together your maximum allowable offer. Let's say we're purchasing a property on 123 Main Street. We've got the executor of the property, the seller, offering us the property at $100,000. Now, it's important before you talk to an individual over the phone and set up an appointment to look at the property, or make that second call, that you have all of your numbers locked down. Your comps should be accurate. So, before you head out the door or hop on the phone, have your information in place. Your buyer needs to see you've done your homework and that your numbers make sense.

Once we've selected three really solid comps, we are ready to talk about the ARV. In this example, the ARV is $200,000. Let's say we use 65% after repair value because it's a

Midwestern property. As we start figuring out our numbers, we'll take the $200,000, which is the ARV, and multiply it by 65% to give us a $130,000 starting point. So far, we're good with what we're able to pick up in the deal. We're being offered the property at $100,000. After we subtract and factor in 65%, we're at $130,000, which is a sizeable difference.

We now have to add in our expenses to come up with our maximum allowable offer. Let's say on this deal we want to make a $20,000 profit. That's normally what we like to put in, but it will range from market to market. Some markets might allow you to make more money so that you could swing from $30,000, $40,000, and even $50,000. The MAO is also going to depend on the deal. Since this is an example, I'm just going to stick with a $20,000 profit.

With this part of the deal figured out, we next move onto contracting costs. Let's say we found a contractor from Thumbtack, and they inspected the property with us. They tell us it would cost $30,000 to do everything that's needed to bring the property up to today's trends. If they give me a $28,000 quote, I'll pad it and round up to $30,000.

Now we'll add in $600 for insurance, $2,500 for property taxes, and $400 for utilities because if we're rehabbing the property, we're going to need to keep utilities on so the work can be done throughout the house. Note that the utilities might also be paid for by the ultimate end buyer, but if not, include the cost.

Now, we'll add in the inspection. If we're selling the property to a retail buyer or cash buyer, they're going to need to inspect the property, and we need to have the utilities on for them to properly complete that inspection.

Finally, we want to add in the closing costs. Remember, I am using that $1,500 I talked about earlier. I would double it and you can do the same if you like.

Our next step is where the flipping magic comes in. When we subtract all the costs, we have an MAO of $75,000. This means we've got to do some negotiations with the executor of the estate. Now, when we're doing our negotiations, I always like to find out the seller's "why" for why they want to sell the property. As you know, we're not in this business to be salespeople. We're real estate investors. The one thing I will tell you not to skip is always finding out the seller's whys, or their motivations. We've already found out somebody in the family passed away. Let's say in this example, mom passed away and left the property to the heirs. Let's assume we're talking to Jim, the executor. He has yet to talk to his brothers, Billy and Robert, so they can all feel good about how they are handling Mom's house. Before any deal can be written, these three brothers have to talk and make sure everything's good to go.

We also need to find out the answers to a few questions about these sons, so we know our next steps. Where are they located? Are they located in the state? Are they located in other parts of the country? Do they have the cash for the $30,000 to get the property up to where they want to sell it at top dollar? We need to find out what their problems are. Obviously, one of the problems is that Mom just passed away. But we need more information about their situation than that. I want to know and will ask them: "Why are you wanting to sell?" I would say to them,

"Imagine we're walking through the property. Tell me what you would start doing to the property. Imagine I gave you a $25,000 Lowe's gift card, and you could do whatever you wanted to the property with that $25,000. What would you start doing?"

When I say this, I am getting them to open up and say, "I would do the kitchen. I would do the bathrooms. I would do the carpets. I would repaint the walls. The roof is leaking, so I would redo that."

What just happened? Suddenly, you've learned about a plethora of items that need attention in the property. That's when you can start saying, "One of the things we can do, since this is what we specialize in as a real estate investor, is you wouldn't have to pay those costs to fix up this property. You wouldn't have to worry about those burdens anymore or knowing something could go wrong with the roof and cause severe damage to the interior of the property and the exterior, of course. When roofs cause damage, it's costly sometimes. We're willing to come in, fix up the property, and get it back to what it should be to sell it in today's market."

As long as you explain things the right way, and find out their problems, you'll have a much smoother transaction. Instead of pulling, old-school 1970s car salesman tricks and tips and other mind-meld stuff, I become a problem-solver. When you become a problem-solver, you can help people. That's what we're in this business for, to help people. Yes, we're obviously in the business to make money. But, if you're not solving people's problems, you're not making money. Always find out the problems. The problem isn't just that they lost a loved one. Yeah, that's a huge, huge stress on them. It takes time to mourn. But we want to help solve their problems right now with solutions to the property. This approach also makes sense because most probate properties are extremely outdated. This puts you in the prime position to be the problem solver and to alleviate pain. Come up with solutions to the problems, and you're golden.

Under Contract

We'll continue with our scenario and assume we get the property under contract at $75,000. We're now in a position to work with the title company and perform another part of our due diligence. Don't forget; you do not want to send off a title request until you've secured an end buyer. I've known several people who have done this, and they've ruined relationships with their title company provider because they've sent them five, 10, and 15 purchase and sales agreements that never closed. So, cool your jets on contacting the title company until you are 100% certain you have a solid cash buyer in play.

Once you get a signed agreement in place, the title needs to be ordered. Now, title work typically takes about three to five business days to complete. Again, some counties are going to be different. If you're in a big metropolitan area, it could take a day. It could take two days. In areas like the Midwest, it typically takes between two to five days, depending on the county and how quickly they can get the information to us.

It makes sense to double-check with your title company for what's needed and their timeframes as well. If you're in an attorney-close state, contact the title company or the attorney to ask what they need from you to process your request of ordering title. In most cases, it's the purchase and sales agreement. If you're going to be wholesaling, an assignment contract will be needed, too. Don't worry, if you don't have experience with writing or interpreting contracts. We're talking contracts in the next chapter on exit strategies. For the most part, the title company will ask for a purchase and sales agreement because all the terms of the deal are included in those docs. Plus, your assignment contract is also going to state how much profit you're going to make. This also goes on the closing statement, so you will receive that check or wire when the deal is finished.

Next step: make sure the executors of the estate don't analyze the title work. It's not their responsibility anyway. Although, it is their duty to analyze what debts, liens, or collections remain from their mother or whoever passed. It is our job to do the analysis. Once the title work is done, I always ask for the title report because you want to make sure the owner of record on the title is the right person to deal with because the only person who can legally sell me the property is the person on title, also called the owner of record. If the individual is unable to do the closing, they may have in place a limited power of attorney (LPOA) or a power of attorney (POA). The LPOA gives a person a limited role, which is more than likely just signing closing documentation. The POA gives the person power, as stated in the document, to execute legal documents per the assignee. When a person or business owns rights to the property, and then give those rights to another person or business, they are known as an assignor. The person granted the rights is called the assignee. Assigning rights to property is quite common, and when it occurs, the assignor is allowed to place restrictions on how the assignee can use the property. Before property can be assigned, a contract will need to be created. This contract should name the person or entity who is receiving rights to the property.

In some cases, the executor of the state hasn't done a quitclaim deed quite yet, so you want to make sure the person that passed is still in the position as an owner of record on the title. You also want to make sure you have the right documentation for the executor to sign by using what's called a power of attorney.

Also, be sure there aren’t any existing liens. If there are existing liens, you need to know those are going to be paid off, and they're not going to be your problem moving forward. There could be mortgages. There could be judgments or collections. You need to make sure those are all taken care of before you acquire the property. Say, for example, we do end up executing a contract. We purchase it for $75,000, and everything's going to be paid off through the executor. The executor is using the proceeds from the $75,000 to pay off all those liens. Then, once that happens, we'll have what's called a free and clear title, which is what our end buyer wants.

Once we have looked at the title report, all the info is correct, and there are no outstanding taxes on the property, municipality liens, or federal tax liens, everything's good to go. If these are not paid off, there could be potential problems. Work with your title company on any outstanding liens that are out of the norm, so you can properly move forward and close without a ripple.

The Closing Process

The first thing you will want to find out when you are working with the title company is how much time they need to close. Typically they're going to want one or maybe two days. Whatever their time frame, make sure you give them the time they need because this is going to be a relationship you're going to have moving forward. You don't want to jeopardize it by trying to rush them. If you don't need to rush, don't. Set up the closing date. If you're going to be doing this as a wholesale transaction, make sure you set it up, so everything's in place. Are you going to be needed at the closing? Surprise! No, you're not. If you're going to be doing an assignment of contract transaction, you especially don't need to be there. Instead, you can send wire instructions to the title company, and they can wire your money to you that same day.

I always recommend the wire over other methods of receiving your money. There's no reason to get a check and then post it on Facebook and say, "This is what I did." If you want to do that, yeah, it's exciting because it's your first deal, but if you're already doing deals, just get the wire. It's fast, it's easy, and it clears your account on the same day in most cases. You don't have to worry about cashing a check that takes five to seven days to clear because there might be a hold on it. Just make sure everything is set up for the executor of the estate: the power of attorney, the closing appointment, and that our ultimate end buyer has signed where they needed to on all of the documentation.

If you're doing this yourself, then make sure everything's coordinated properly. Or if you've got a closing coordinator on your team, they can set up everything you need. If you need more information on how to structure your business, my first book, *Right Flipping Now* goes in-depth on how to run a business, set up your standard operation procedures, and the roles and responsibilities of each of your team members.

After all is said and done, we're ready to get to work. Turn the page and let's get started working on actual deals for you!

CHAPTER SEVEN: GO TIME

It's time for us to start putting together deals and making profit spreads.

In this chapter, we're going to cover the exit strategies you can use for every single deal you do. Whether you're working on your first probate deal or your 20th, you can use these strategies.

Before you implement any of these upcoming strategies, talk to an attorney about the strategies you can use and the different ways they will be implemented. Your attorney will give you the green light on being able to execute. California, Texas, and a few other states have different documentation criteria, and you need your attorney to be your advisor to make sure you are correctly conducting business. Whatever states you are doing business in, you need to ensure that you adhere to the requirements, so you don't get in trouble.

With the legal mumbo jumbo out of the way, we are ready to explore the different kinds of transactions.

Assignment Contract

Transacting a deal using an assignment contract is simple.

In the previous chapter, we covered a basic example of adding profit into your deal and being able to pull that profit out at closing. That's one way to structure a deal.

In our example, the seller is the owner of record and the executor of the estate. They're handling everything because they have a power of attorney and are signing on behalf of the deceased. You will be the investor in the contract. The reason I advised you to line up your cash buyers in previous chapters, is because when you do have the opportunity for a deal, you can seize it since your cash buyers are at the ready for you to sign the deal over to them, or in more official terms, assign the contract. In this exit strategy, you will need a cash buyer and an alternate buyer.

Here are the ins and outs of this contract type and, in particular, the six steps you need to take within this particular exit strategy.

Step 1

You agree to terms with the owner—the executor of the estate.

Step 2

Execute the purchase and sales agreement.

Again, I recommend that you use your state-approved purchasing sales agreement. It's clean. It's been approved by your state's attorneys and your state's board of realtors, so you don't need to worry about missing any critical elements. Use that state-approved purchasing sales agreement, and you're good to go.

Step 3

You have found an end buyer who's ready to buy the contract.

Step 4

Sign the assignment contract.

If you're wondering how to get your hands on an assignment contract, later in this book, I share my resources to help you out. Your attorney can review your assignment contract to make sure every legality has been handled.

Step 5

Schedule a time for the closing.

As we've discussed in the due diligence chapter, as soon as your end buyer signs the deal, you need to order the title. If you want to have a quick closing, get the title work ordered.

Step 6

This is the easiest step. You are collecting your assignment fee from the closed transaction, which will be in the form of a check or wire—this is all based on what you want to do. My company always does wires, but if this is going to be your first payout, get a check. It's a cool experience, especially for your first deal. Take a picture of it and put it up in your office. Let it be a symbol of what you have just accomplished—something not a lot of people do. Many people say they're going to do it, but they don't follow up their words with the action you're taking. Don't discount yourself with a pat on the back. Closing your first deal is huge! I want you to savor the experience and remember it every time you look at that check on the wall.

Executing the Steps

Once the purchase and sales agreement has been signed with the owner of record and you have an executed agreement binding you to the terms put forth in the contract, this is where things get exciting and real. You're now that much closer to getting a deal to the closing table.

On the purchase and sales agreement, where it says "buyer," put your company name. If you're going to be operating as a sole proprietor, make sure the agreement reflects that. Then you're going to include "and/or assigns" after your company name. For example, if we're using my company, the agreement will read "No Flipping Excuses LLC and/or assigns." This is relevant when executing the assignment exit strategy. This language needs to be added to the buyer line, which you need to complete. The only other way around that is if you had an attorney put together a special purchase and sales agreement noting the specific language in a section of the contract that gives you the rights to assign the deal.

Remember, if you want a smooth closing, you need to order the title immediately upon the execution of both the purchasing sales agreement and the assignment contract.

Envision this deal unfolding in this way: the homeowner, who is the owner of record, will have a contract put together with you (i.e., the purchase and sales agreement). In that agreement, you have the right to assign contract to the property or purchase it. In this case, we're going to assign the property. The individual that will be purchasing the deal from you as the investor will be using an assignment contract. Meaning, there will be two legally executed contracts in place: the purchase and sales agreement between you and the homeowner, aka the owner of record, and the assignment contract between you and your investor—who is providing cash to close so that you can get paid. The ultimate buyer is going to purchase the property and will give you, the investor, non-refundable earnest money per the details outlined by you—the investor—on the assignment contract. This is a non-refundable EMD, which stands for earnest money deposit, and will reflect on the closing statement.

Your purchase and sales agreement between the executor of the estate, the owner of record, and you require an earnest money deposit. If you don't have the $500 or $1,000 or the amount listed in the terms in the contract, you need to disclose that immediately. It is feasible to arrange to pay this money in chunks; in other words, you don't have to come up with the money all at once. Regardless of the terms, I recommend you opt for the non-refundable portion arrangement.

A non-refundable portion arrangement allows for some of the non-refundable earnest money deposit to be allocated to the owner of record per the language detailed in the purchase and sales agreement. The assignment contract must be given to the title and escrow company for proper fee disbursement. You can pay this with a check or wire.

Now, this is just one transaction, and remember, our wholesale deal is comprised of two transactions. What we are discussing is an A to C (that is, assign to contract). No closing costs fees have to be paid from you or your portions of the profit.

The best thing you can do to bypass providing earnest money deposits is have your end buyer provide them. When they pay it, it can sit at your title company or in your attorney's escrow account. These funds will be verified from your seller—the executor of the estate.

As you can see, the assignment contract is very easy to use, and we've only introduced it to you in this chapter. We will be talking about it more toward the end of this chapter. Let's move on to the next exit strategy.

Wholesaling with a Joint Venture (JV) Agreement

Let's say you come across a great opportunity, and you want to get rid of the deal, but you don't have a buyer specifically for that area. Well, the best thing to do is still put it out to your list. Maybe include a list of some other wholesalers, too.

In this instance, there would be a JV agreement and an assignment contract in place.

If you're going to do the JV agreement, you and the other party need to decide what the split will be. I typically do a 50/50 spread. If I've put together a JV agreement with the seller and my wholesaler puts together the deal with an ultimate end buyer, in my eyes, that's doing 50/50 of the work. I have no problem splitting that fee with the other individual.

Wholesaling JV Steps

There are seven steps you need to take within this particular exit strategy.

Step 1

Your seller is the executor of the state. You are going to be the investor. There will also be an investor partner and your ultimate cash buyer—who is buying the deal. This is your deal since you found it, and you and the executor have come to terms by this point. Your purchase and sales agreement will be in place.

Step 2

Make sure the document is signed, and the assigns on the purchase and sales agreement are complete in every area that requires it.

Step 3

With your end buyer in place from your JV, make sure you have your joint venture agreement in place. Between steps two and three, make sure you have agreed to terms that are completely laid out in the joint venture agreement. If you don't have access to a joint venture agreement, I'll share with you ways you can get your hands on that document.

Step 4

Make sure you have the assignment contract fully executed. Now, when you are first getting into probates, there might be confusion over who is going to be on the assignment contract. The company of the person who signed the purchase and sales agreement with the executor of the estate will be on the assignment contract. This is important to note: the person who brought in the buyer will not be on the contract; they will still get paid though. Their names will go on the settlement statement. Makes sure the business entity or the sole proprietor on the purchase and sales agreement will be the same party on the assignment contract.

Step 5

All agreements will be sent to the title company, and the title is pulled. If this is your deal, make sure the title company knows of the joint venture agreement and that the assignment fee is being split between you and your JV partner per the JV agreement terms. After the title comes back and everything is clear, we move on to the next step.

Step 6

Schedule the closing.

If the executor is out of state, you will do a remote closing where everything is still signed, but all parties are not present. Once signed, the ultimate end buyer on the assignment contract would make sure all the legal documents that have to be recorded have been.

Step 7

It's time for the closing. Both investors receive a distribution of profits that have been agreed to on the joint venture agreement. Here's the breakdown: Your partner can bring you a deal, or they will bring you a cash buyer for the transactions. The roles in this agreement should be equal. There will still be a purchase and sales agreement and an assignment contract in place.

A side note on closing: never assume the title has been ordered until you ask. If you have the option, I always encourage the seller to go through our title company as there will be fewer fees. We do transactions with a specific title company every month, and it just makes the whole process easier since everyone is familiar with everyone else. If one of the parties has an attorney, they want to use, that's fine. Just make sure you know all of the transactions will take place at the one closing.

At this point, the joint venture agreement is in place. The parameters of how much each investor will be making, once the transaction closes successfully, have been agreed upon. Once the deal is closed, you will receive your share of the profits. You can pick up a check or have the check mailed to you. If you don't want a check, then you can request your money to be wired.

A typical joint venture agreement will be set for even distribution, to be split at closing. Meaning, if there's a $20,000 assignment fee, both parties will receive a $10,000 spread on that deal. Now, if you bring a seller and your JV brings the buyer or vice versa, that is a 50/50 deal. Each individual will be paid from the B to C transaction (i.e., the contract between the real estate investor and the ultimate buyer), and separate checks or wires will be given to each sole proprietor and/or their business entity.

If you don't have the funds right now to set up a business entity, then do the deal and set up your business later. Remember, this is a business, not a hobby. The sooner your business is set up, the sooner you will be able to escape your nine to five. Or if you've already escaped the nine to five, congratulations to you. In any regard, this is an item that goes at the top of your priority list.

Wholesaling for Quick Cash

If you are in a state that might not allow the use of an assignment contract, I recommend you take another tack to avoid fees and having to pay for a hard money lender, a private money lender, or that you use transactional money. You can solve this issue by using our escrow agreement with your wholesale transactions.

This is what we call an A to B, B to C transaction, and it just means there will be two transactions within this deal, and both will take place on one day. This deal is very similar to what we do with our assignment contract, but in the A to B, B to C transaction, there will not be an assignment contract.

I'll simplify this transaction as much as possible. A is going to be the executor of the estate. B is going to be you, the investor. C is going to be your ultimate cash buyer—who you will make your profit from.

Wholesaling for Quick Cash Steps

There are six steps you need to take within this particular exit strategy.

Step 1

Agree to terms with the owner, the executor of the estate.

Step 2

Execute the purchase and sales agreement.

Step 3

Find a cash buyer to sell the subject property to.

Step 4

You've found a cash buyer, and the deal is created. There will be a separate purchase and sales agreement in place—this is the B to C contract part of this transaction. Remember, B is the investor, which is you. C is going to be your ultimate end buyer.

Step 5

The B to C contract is executed.

To recap: At this point, we have the purchase and sales agreement—one between the owner of record, aka the executor of the estate, and us. We also have a second agreement in place—called the B to C, where we are the seller, selling the deal to our ultimate end buyer.

Step 6

The end buyer signs what's called an escrow agreement at closing.

This is the breakdown of wholesaling for a quick cash transaction. You're going to have two separate purchase and sales agreements that are going to be in place for the A to B and B to C transactions. The title work will be ordered immediately after you secure the end buyer. The earnest money you need for the A to B contract comes from your B to C contract.

The end buyer will pay double what the earnest money is from your A to B contract. Upon receipt of the earnest money deposit from the C buyer, the funds shall be deposited into the title company's escrow account. Verification of funds for A—the owner—can be made to satisfy that requirement.

Earnest money deposit from the end buyer is always non-refundable. They're purchasing the property in as-is condition, so they are on the hook. The only way they can get their earnest money back is if we fail to disclose information on the title report. They should know if something's wrong with the actual house—the subject property—they won't get their funds back.

The escrow agreement will be signed by the end buyer, acknowledging that their funds will be used to fund your A to B contract. On the escrow agreement, the end buyer doesn't know why we're purchasing the property. All they know is they're getting a slam-dunk deal from us and that their funds are being used for the contract between the executor of the estate and us. We are fully transparent with them that their funds are going to be used for our A to B; they will never know how much we're purchasing the property for. Even though we don't disclose this information, they can find it by looking at the record after closing. If they have an issue with the amount at that time, they can't dispute it because they've already bought the property.

I don't tell you this to be shady. I always encourage that if you're getting a great deal, give that deal away as a great deal—especially to your cash buyers. You want to make them happy. The happier they are, the happier you'll be because they will be buying deals from you—left and right.

I'd rather have a deal done multiple times with one buyer than have one deal done for a large profit spread—and then that party and I never do a deal again. I like to build relationships. And this is important to think about because, in this business, we are in it for the long haul. If you give a person a deal that's not super rock solid, they're more than likely not going to come back to you to do any more deals. If they do, they're going to negotiate the heck out of deals from you, and you don't want to deal with that situation or dynamic. Those deals are big stressful pains in the butt. This is the last complication you want in your business.

Bypassing the Earnest Money Deposit Timeline

Yes, you can use specific language in your purchase and sales agreement to bypass the earnest money deposit that is normally due within 24 to 48 hours after you sign and execute your A to B contract.

This language will normally go on the second to last page of your state's purchase and sales agreement.

This is verbatim, the language we use:

"The buyer will deliver the earnest money deposit to the escrow company three days before the set closing date."

In this case, we also add the following language:

"The buyer may cancel the purchase of the subject property due to title report, inspection, survey, and or appraisal report."

This is our out, so if something comes back on the title that we don't like, we have an exit strategy—within an exit strategy.

You hardly ever find any issues when dealing with probates, but a small percentage of deals will show liens. When this is the case, you don't want to move forward with that particular deal. You want a safety net to get you out of it.

Since there is no assignment contract on this deal, you will have a B to C end buyer purchase and sales agreement. This states the buyer is purchasing the property in as-is condition, and the earnest money deposit will be non-refundable. We want to include this language, so our deal is tight, and there is no way for the buyer to exit it unless we've failed to disclose something like a title deficiency. The title deficiency happens when the title report gives us a breakdown of several potential problems such as mechanics liens, federal/state tax liens, a collection that's turned into a judgment, first, second, or third mortgage, home equity line of credit (HELOC), municipality lien, code violations, unpaid property taxes, incorrect owners of record reflecting, foreclosure judgments, HOA judgments, lawsuits and anything else that can be legally attached to the property as a lien. These are the most common, and the majority of them can be taken off of title to help give you a free and clear property. But if there is a title issue that can't be resolved, you don't want to mess around with it unless it can be cleared up within a very short period. When I see title issues, I will make an exception to exiting the deal if I know the title will be cleared in one or two days. If it's going to take months, I will back away as quickly as possible.

Assuming we are going forward and there are no title issues, then all funds shall be verified, and deposited in the title company's escrow account on the morning of closing. If you're using an attorney, you will also transact your closing in this way.

I always encourage people to let the ultimate end-buyer know when the closing will be and when the funds need to wired. Usually, I send a simple message to them, stating: "Hey, this is what time we're closing. Make sure you have funds wired the day before, so we have a smooth transaction." Yes, they should know this information, and no, you are not responsible for telling them any of the above. It does give you peace of mind to know that you can confirm the ultimate end buyer has received the pertinent information to allow your deal to go through—because you have given it to them.

A lot of buyers, unfortunately, will wire the funds the morning of closing, and when this is the case, sometimes we can't collect our checks that same day. That doesn't reflect well to our executor of the estate. And what about if you're working with an attorney and the funds are late? The last thing you want is for the executor to go back to your referral source (the attorney—who could have more deals for you in the pipeline) and say, "We signed all the documents, but I haven't received the funds yet. We're waiting on a wire."

Don't allow this to happen on a Friday. Because if it happens on a Friday, people are going to be waiting until Monday. This is completely unacceptable, and people have a right to be upset that they have to wait on their payout. I don't like having closings on Friday because of this. You can avoid this by making sure you're on the ball, and your title company or escrow officer is calling the end buyer to confirm they have received wire instructions, and that a wire will be going out that same day, or on the date indicated in the instructions.

Wholesaling with Transactional Funding

You will use wholesaling with transactional funds as an exit strategy if the escrow agreement we discussed within the previous exit strategy is not being allowed by your end buyer.

This can happen. You can have an end buyer that you haven't properly vetted, and they might be kind of a jerk. I hate to tell you this, but it is a reality sometimes. After the deal, you may want to assess if you want to do business with them in the future. Once the deal has been agreed to, you need to go forward and get it done. You're likely looking at a profit between $25,000 and $30,000, so do what you need to do to get the deal done.

The same parameters are in place.

A is the owner of record—the executor of the estate. B is you, and you're the investor. C is your ultimate end buyer. Again, we are working with an A to B, B to C transaction.

Wholesaling with Transactional Funding Steps

There are six steps you need to take within this particular exit strategy.

Step 1

Agree to terms with the owner.

Step 2

Execute the purchase and sales agreement between the executor of the estate—A and yourself, as the buyer—B. That's your A to B portion of the deal.

Step 3

After locating an end buyer for your deal, you and the end buyer agree to terms.

Step 4

Execute a purchase and sales agreement with your end buyer.

Now, remember before we get to step 5, and immediately after completing step 4, order your title work. Once that title work is back and everything looks clean, *then* you are ready to move one.

Step 5

Schedule a time to do the closing for each contract.

Your transaction recap: You will have a contract between you and the owner of record, which is the A to B portion. Next, you will have a contract between you and your ultimate end buyer, which is the B to C portion.

Step 6

Funds are sent to the title company from your transactional funder. You will receive either your check or a wire the same day.

Now here's the breakdown:

- You're going to have two separate purchase and sales agreements that are going to be in place for the A to B and B to C transactions.
- Title work is ordered immediately after you secure the end buyer.
- Earnest money for the A to B contract comes from your B to C contract.
- Your end buyer will pay twice. The end buyer will typically pay double the earnest money deposit, so you know they're serious. This also enables you to fulfill your contractual obligations with the owner of

record—you can give them their earnest money from your A to B purchase and sales agreement.

The A to B contract should state the following within the addendum section, which will typically be on the second to last page: "Buyer will deliver earnest money deposit to escrow company three days prior to the set closing date."

If the seller doesn't agree to that, that's completely fine. Everything is 100% negotiable. Find out what their comfort level is and then get it negotiated and into the contract.

Another option for your buyer might be that they will deliver the earnest money to the escrow company 10 days after signing and executing the purchase and sales agreement. This will give you a big enough window to get the earnest money deposit from your ultimate end buyer. Since you should already have this person lined up and ready to go, you can have a brief conversation with them that might go something like: "Hi, I've got this great deal. It's coming up. It's in the area you're buying in, and you'll be able to make a ton of money on it because I'm getting it at a discount. So, I want to sell it to you at a discount."

Next in the agreement, in the addendum section, include: "Buyer may cancel the purchase of subject property due to title report, inspection, survey, and or appraisal." You want that language included in case there is a deficiency in the title, or maybe you do an inspection, survey, or appraisal, and the results are worse than you expected. Make sure you have proper outs so you can exit from any deal that turns up non-negotiable information without being out your earnest money deposit.

The B to C contract will state: "Buyer is purchasing the property in as-is condition, and the earnest money deposit will be non-refundable. All funds shall be verified deposited in title company's escrow account the morning of closing." I can't stress enough that the funds need to be there when they are expected to be there. You don't want to be caught with your pants down on a Friday without funds. It's not a good way to do business.

So if this is your first time working with a cash buyer, do not close on a Friday; close on a Monday, and no later than a Thursday. When you select these days to close, if the funds are delayed, you can still get everything taken care of. If funds come in late on a Thursday, you can get everything wrapped up the next day—as long as it's not a holiday.

About Earnest Money Deposit Amounts

Here's a question I hear a lot, and it also applies to each of these exit strategies. How much is a normal earnest money deposit?

It depends on the amount of the house you're buying. The amount of the earnest money deposit will mainly be predicated on the purchase price. The higher the price you're paying for the home, the more an owner of record will want to see good faith. A good rule of thumb is that you will pay 1-3% for the deposit, which will be stated on the purchase and sales agreement. Keep in mind, this amount can be 100% negotiable and may not fall into the 1-3% range. On homes less than $250,000, we'll typically put down between $500 to $2,000, and that number solely depends on how comfortable we are with moving that property. Normally on homes $250,000 or higher, it's much more acceptable to be closer to the 1% mark. The only time we've used a higher rate is on bulk property packages.

Let's say I put $1,000 earnest money deposit down on the purchase and sales agreement; I'm going to ask for $2,000 from my ultimate end buyer for the earnest money deposit. That will cover my A to B contract and even allow me a little bit of a cushion in case something goes wrong.

For properties between $200,000 to $500,000, the earnest money deposit can be anywhere between $1,500 and $3,500. My rule of thumb is once you go over a certain amount, the earnest money will range between 1-3%. You need to figure out what you are comfortable with putting down since you will need to have your cash ready, so you can proceed forward and execute.

Understand, the earnest money deposit doesn't go into your pocket. It goes to the escrow account at either the title company or your attorney. The funds will be verified by your seller, the owner of record—the executor of the estate. On your purchase and sales agreement with your ultimate end buyer, their earnest money is a non-refundable deposit.

Locating Funding

If you need help finding a transactional funding company, I recommend that our students use my point-of-contact. I know the owner extremely well. He's even been on our podcast. If you haven't listened to our show before, it's called the No Flipping Excuses Show. You can find us on iTunes or YouTube. You will get to know all about the owner of this company, and then you can decide for yourself if you want to use him.

The company we recommend and that we have been using for years is called Best Transaction Funding. The owner's name is Duane Ortega. Best Transaction Funding has some of the lowest fees in the entire industry. I've never had anybody complain that they haven't received their money. No one has ever complained about them period. If you want to check them out, head over to their website—www.besttransactionfunding.com, and let them know I sent you. When you get in contact with them, you will receive an opportunity to receive a discount on your processing fee.

This process is really simple. Just fill out an intake form requesting for funds to close on both A to B and B to C transactions. You can request an unlimited proof of funds (POF) letter on their website if you need one. It's free. Now, if you're not going to use these folks, don't take advantage of what they are offering. When you do use them, you can expect the smoothest transactions with nothing to worry about.

I want to give you the confidence you need to go out there and execute one of these exit strategies.

To do so, you need to be aware of the documentation you need and that we have talked about in this chapter. Head on over to www.noflippingexcuses.com/probate-contracts to find the contracts you need. All I ask is that you enter your email address and first name, so we know you're the person requesting the information.

Review these documents with your attorney because each state has different laws and processes. Make sure you are aware of how your transactions will go down. These documents will help you get your deals done quickly and easily.

Our next and final chapter contains the bonus material I've been telling you about.

I put it together, specifically because it is going to be a game-changer when you execute the probates strategies in this book. I'm covering more tips and tricks to closing probate deals that will allow you to separate yourself even more from the competition in your area.

Make sure you read it, to gain the edge in your business.

CHAPTER EIGHT: PROBATE BONUS POINTS

Congratulations!

You've made it!

Most people will never hear about the information in this chapter. If you've read all seven chapters, now you're ready for the bonus information.

I've only shared this information with our top coaching students. This is a strategy that not everybody is going to use because not everybody has this book. We're doing only a limited release, so we're not going to be selling thousands and thousands of copies. I'm not planning on becoming a New York Times Bestseller. I simply want to get this information into the hands of people who want to help change people's lives by offering what not everybody can—that's you coming in and helping them during a very difficult time.

Pre-Probate Strategy

With the pre-probate strategy, you're relieving a burden on executors of estates. They don't want to place a burden on the heir. A lot of people, when they know that life is nearing the end, don't want to place burdens on people. They want to leave being happy, but obviously, it is a very sad and emotional time. Having gone through this with family members and friends, I can say it is a very difficult and tragic period of life. But, if we can help folks out and ease the burden when they are making that transition, or maybe when they are still full of life, that's a great gift to bring to the table.

A pre-probate strategy happens when the owner of record for either a residential or commercial property is not deceased. The subject property changes title to a new status without the deceased party on the deed.

Here's an example. Let's say Maryanne and Jeff have been married for the past 50 years, and Jeff passes away. Well, Maryanne now has this big old property, and she has no idea what to do with it. Her son and daughters say, "Mom, why don't we go through the process of trying to get you moved into an assisted living facility, or you can come live with us?" That's normally the case when a husband and wife have been together for a very long time, and one of them passes. The one left behind is going to end up decluttering the house and wanting to move or wanting to go into an assisted living facility. They might move in with a son, daughter, or another relative.

When somebody passes away, a death certificate has to be created. The spouse or executor of the estate receives the death certificate. This allows them to do a quitclaim deed—which removes a person from the title. When this happens, a notification is sent out, reading something along the lines of: "The deed has now been transferred to the(individual's name)." In this case, it would be Maryanne, who would receive the property that is now under her name. The title of her home won't include her and her husband anymore. When this QCD is filed, you can gain access to this information. This is an opportunity to contact Maryanne to see if she wants to sell.

From my previous experience in doing this for a very long time, Maryanne now has this big four-bedroom, two-and-a-half bath house. It’s just her in the home now. She's getting a little bit older, and she doesn't want to maintain or keep the property anymore. Maybe she doesn’t know how to do that. Most of the time, her son or daughter will help out; they want to take care of Mom. This should be the top priority. Selling is not a priority. Whatever the case, we want to make sure Mom feels good about her life. If we can ease the burden and come in and make an offer on this property and make Mom’s transition to a new life from that house easier, we definitely should. The family might want to sell a ton of personal property to you as well.

From my experience, the majority of pre-probate transactions are free and clear. A lot of times, there are no mortgages to deal with, and if there are, they are minimal. People have been living in the house for 20, 30, and 40 years. This puts them and you in a good position. Normally on these types of properties, they're below a 50% loan-to-value, LTV—on any mortgage liens placed upon the property.

An affidavit of death, aka AOD, is created when someone has passed away. The title shows the co-owner or spouse as the sole owner of record at the time a certificate of death has been recorded.

The subject property doesn't enter into probate, as the title has a living, willing, and able owner of record. The majority of the time, the individual left as the owner of record of the subject property wants to sell their property due to potential trauma and or the discomfort of being left in the property alone. Let's assume Maryanne's in her early 60s, and her husband's passing is untimely.

Maybe Maryanne doesn't want to go to an assisted living facility. Maybe she wants to sell the property and downgrade to a two-bedroom, one-bath. A lot of individuals don't want to live in their present house anymore, but they *do* want a house. Maybe they don't want the upkeep. They don't want to mow the lawn. They don't want to worry about the exterior of the property. They might want to live in a retirement community and have the landscaping taken care of. They want to make sure they're in a house that doesn't require a lot of exterior maintenance. Their motivation levels to sell are extremely high due to the household income dropping from two-income providers to one. In most cases, the sole individual isn't working anymore.

Maryanne might be working part-time while also receiving social security benefits every single month. If Jeff just passed away and he was also working part-time plus had a retirement fund every month from his pension, he also had social security benefits coming in. Since he's passed, his social security is going to be gone. He could have left behind the retirement pension, depending on how the pension is set up for the remaining spouse of survivorship. If that's the case, she might still be receiving it, but there could also be nothing left.

Let's say the mortgage is paid off, and she doesn't want to live there. She owns the house free and clear. She knows she could take her money and buy a smaller house. There would be enough money left over to live comfortably in her remaining years. Since most folks retire in their early 60s, if you want to retire comfortably with you and your spouse to live another 20, 30 years after retirement, you need to have anywhere between $2.5 to $3 million in your bank. Barring that, you need to have recurring revenue every single month. This might take the form of rental income, stocks, bonds, IRAs, etc.

Unfortunately, most Americans do not have near that amount of money sitting in their bank account, and they don't usually have assets that pay them monthly. If, in this case, Jeff did have a few apartment buildings, Maryanne would still be receiving that money. They own those properties. Still, we'll assume this couple didn't have any money in their bank. If you come in and help the family, Maryanne can move closer to her family. They can go out and be more active. You're helping to give folks peace of mind when you give Maryanne a solution. This is their light at the end of the tunnel.

Finding the AOD

An AOD is recorded through the county recorder's office and can be found in recent cases through the clerk's office when people pass away. You will not see the probate papers in the file, but you can find out who has recently passed away.

If you don't want to go to the recorder's office, you can locate notices of death through a Google search.

An attorney referral is helpful here, as well, so circle through your sphere of influence. An attorney is going to deal directly with beneficiaries. In this case, maybe Maryanne's talked to her attorney and said, "I'm thinking of moving." Of course, the attorney is going to try and help Maryanne to the best of their ability. If you are in with the attorney, they might say to Maryanne: "I've got this investor. They're looking for properties in the area, so if you want to, you could receive a fast and fair cash offer."

Of course, the attorney is representing his client and wants to do right by her. So he will look out for her.

In our example, Maryanne and Jeff have been living in their house for 30 to 40 years, and it hasn't been updated once—which translates to a lot of money going out the door for the buyer/investor. Maybe the roof hasn't had been maintained in 10-plus years; maybe there are other problems. We need to know all about them. After all, Mom just lost her husband of 30-plus years, so let's be a problem solver and tell her: "We're willing to do all the work to the house and give you a very fast and fair cash offer." Having this attorney on your side could bring you some sizeable deals and profits.

When you find out the AOD information, you might not be able to find the contact information you need. You can get access to an address easily by doing a skip trace—and again, I recommend using fastpeoplesearch.com. You can also use a software called ReboGateway—www.rebogateway.com. We don't receive an affiliate commission if you decide to sign up with them. If you create an account, know they do receive information directly from the county. They allow you to see recently filed quick claim deeds. Timing is of the essence in these instances because if you can get these properties early on, you can get them at substantial, deep discounts.

ReboGateway is a software you purchase. Whether you have done a deal or not, you can receive the information you need, and won't have to go down to the clerk's office. Start building up your sphere of influence, especially attorneys, then go ahead and check out the software for 30-60 days to see if you like it and want to use it in your business.

Your title company can also help you find recently filed quitclaim deeds. If you haven't done any deals with them, they are not going to be thrilled to provide you with information, or they might not want to do deals with you at all. You need to do some business with them before you start asking for the information you need. Of course, they would feel this way. They haven't worked any deals with you. They don't know who you are or how you work. So, they don't have any confidence that you're going to close deals with them. Close some deals before you ask the title company for too much free information.

Marketing to Your AOD

Let's say you've put together a list of potential AODs. When you first get started, your list isn't going to be huge. It will be a similar size to your monthly probates. So, depending on the size of the town or county where you live, you might have 50; or you might get 100 AODs. Some months, you might reach 200. We talked about how to find the information you need to contact people who are left holding the house after a death in the family. When you find out their information, it's time to reach out. Send them a text message; call them on the phone; send them a ringless voicemail or an email broadcast if you can find their email address. You can use direct mail, and the service I referenced—Yellow Letter. Send a postcard if you wish. If you do opt to send direct mail, you will want to read on to find out the type of direct mail pieces that are most effective.

Don't discount the power of the leave-behind either. If you're doing any door-knocking, you could leave behind a Post-it note. It may not sound like it would work, but the leave-behind is one of the key tactics that have helped my team and me over the years. If we're having a difficult time getting ahold of somebody and they are still living at the property, put a nice yellow Post-it note on their door and follow this formula: The top line is going to be in all caps and say, "Important." The next line will say, "Please call me!" Make sure you use that exclamation point. The third line is your phone number. Finally, the fourth line says, "Thanks, Jason."

Make sure you put this message on a regular size Post-it note. Don't use an extra-large one where people can see what is on the note. You want people to be curious about the note and need to walk up to it to ensure that they see it. When they pull up to their driveway, they're going to think, *oh, what's that on my door*? Then they'll go read it and will be intrigued because it says "important" on it." Believe it or not, this simple strategy gives us anywhere between a 65-70% call back ratio from people wondering what we put on their door and why. Using the Post-it note method gives you a high response rate. If you have a low marketing budget right now, this is a great opportunity for you to door-knock and put Post-it notes on people's doors.

If you use Yellow Letter to find out information on probates, you can do the same thing with AODs. You'll note that nowhere in our marketing so far, have we talked about people who have passed. This is why Yellow Letters—yellowletterscomplete.com is an awesome resource. When you send out correspondence, you can use this format: week one is going to be, "Dear, (their first name)" For our purposes, we'll use Maryanne again. So, we would say, "Dear Maryanne, I was driving by your house at 123 Main Street, and I am interested in possibly buying it. If you have any interest in selling, please call me at (555) 555-5555. Sincerely, Jason Lucchesi. PS: I am not a real estate broker. I am just looking to buy it." This works because it is very short, sweet, and straight to the point. This is not a full-page document that will cause them to lose interest or get bored with too much information. You don't want to lose them, so get right to the point.

Give it a full seven days before you send out the next batch. Week two will be, "Dear Maryanne. Hi, my name is Jason, and I am interested in buying your house at 123 Main Street. Please call me at (555) 555-5555. Thanks, Jason." Again, my message is straight to the point. But as we start to progress, we want to take the people who do call us off our list. Move them right along, so we don't keep sending them emails. On the flip side, we also don't want to send people more information when they don't want it.

Week three's correspondence will say: "Dear Maryanne, I'm surprised that I haven't heard from you. I'm still interested in buying your house at 123 Main Street. Please call me at (555) 555-5555. Thanks, Jason. Lucchesi." To reiterate, I'm saying, "Hey, I haven't heard from you," because I'm trying to come across as interested and not pushy. I don't want Maryanne to think I don't care about her. I want her to give me a call. If she's not interested, she'll let me know for sure.

When we strike the right note, they will get the vibe that we're a little surprised they haven't given us a call. Remember, as you plan your marketing that your success lies in the touches of your marketing pieces. That's where most people fail. They send off week one, and if they don't get the response they want, they give up.

I have found that you will receive high response rates from this method, and I highly recommend you keep up with it, especially in weeks one through four. That's where the money is made.

I think the reason for this is simple. This person you are reaching out to just lost somebody. They may have been married 20, 30, 40, or 50-plus years. They may want to talk over their options with an attorney. Maybe they received your letter and now, don't know what to do and need to be assured they are making the right decision. They want to get some help. They want professional advice or to talk it over with their son, daughter, or whomever. This is an important and life-changing decision, and everybody always has some family member they want to discuss financial considerations with.

Week number four is more than likely going to be our last piece. We're going to say, "Dear Maryanne, I am still very interested in purchasing your house at 123 Main Street. Please call me at (555) 555-5555. Thanks, Jason Lucchesi." We're letting her know we're still very interested in purchasing the property, but after that, we're going to put them on a 30-day notice.

Tips to Improve Your Responses

We've tested several hundreds of thousands of direct mail pieces since I've been in the business since 2008.

The following is a successful option that will work if you want to use letters. Buy invitation-style envelopes; they typically come in colors like a light blue or light pink. You see these pastel colors during Easter. Next, put the address of the property on the front with a stamp—and don't use a computer-generated stamp either. Those do not have the same open rate. On the back flap, put your return address, and don't seal it shut. Tuck in the back flap. People feel like this a personal touch, and your envelope stands a greater chance of getting opened. We've seen very, very big success rates from doing direct mailers in this way.

In weeks two, three, or four, get an 8.5x11 manila envelope and put the letter inside. You will not fold this letter. Put the address, return address, and the actual stamps on the front of the envelope. Here's the topper: also, on the front of the envelope, stamp the word "important." Obviously, you are doing this, so they think that what's in the envelope is important and they need to open it. You can even use different types of stamps to persuade them a bit more.

If you are doing a direct response mailer and want a higher rate, wait one week after the final direct mail piece has gone out before you do the leave-behind method, which we just discussed. That's going to be step two in your marketing machine, where you will stop by the house and do the leave behind. Step number three is going to be skip tracing the number of the owner of record. You can also call your contact in weeks 1-4 of your direct mail campaigns to make it a seamless transaction.

Earlier in the book, I gave you access to the scripts we use in our company. You can use the same exact script that you use for calling in your email and direct mail marketing. Start calling your contacts between weeks 6-7 if you haven't heard anything between weeks 1-4. Don't get discouraged if you feel like your efforts aren't working. Getting the results you want is all about consistency.

If you would like access to our direct mailers, go to www.noflippingexcuses.com/aod-marketingpieces. Then you can duplicate the marketing pieces we've covered in this chapter in your business.

Final Flipping Bonus Notes

I hope you found this chapter to be a complete eye-opener. Whenever I share it with our students, they are completely in awe that they have these sorts of options.

The bigger picture is that you can help a person and family out before anything crazy happens with their situations, and they get themselves into a situation they can't recover from. You are giving these people going through such a tragedy, peace of mind. You are helping them move closer to their family and rejoin a community, where they can even thrive eventually after their loss. With you in the picture, they don't have to worry about some big house that's completely outdated.

So go out there, be a helper and a problem solver.

Thank you for reading my book. I want to invite you to reach out to me at our website—www.noflippingexcuses.com if you need any help in getting your business started—or the answers to any questions you might have along the way in developing your business, my team and I are happy to help you.

Finally, you can find the answers to the questions you might have by listening to our podcast, The No Flipping Excuses Show on iTunes. We've recorded over 100 episodes of pure and valuable content. I look forward to hearing from you. If you have a testimonial you would like to send to us about information you found helpful in this book, I would love to hear about it.

I want you to know this business is not easy. I'm sure you've heard the old saying, "If it were easy, everyone would be doing it." That's 100% true. This business isn't easy, and not everyone is doing it. This tells me if I'm willing to work my butt off and continually push myself to my limit daily, I'm going to see the results I desire. Anything rewarding in life is going to take a massive amount of focus. So, put the blinders on and get laser-focused on this business.

Fair warning: as you get going, you'll likely see more failure at first than success. That's okay. You've got to keep the blinders on and push yourself as you've never pushed before. Ignore the negative dipsticks in your life and know there's a light at the end of the tunnel. I was voted least likely to succeed in high school—with a 2.5 GPA. I barely graduated on time, and I have learning disabilities, but I have a work ethic like no other. I strive and thrive when people tell me I can't do this or that. I like proving to myself that I can. The things I've done in this business came from hard work, late nights, blood, sweat, tears, and some days, a straight-up beatdown to where I just wanted to quit. Anyone can quit at anything they do, but it takes a certain kind of person not to quit. Most people who start a new venture, give up after a month. Maybe you've done that in the past. I will tell you right now, as you hold this book in your hands, that is no longer you.

You've made it this far in the book, and I'm proud of you. It's tough for me to finish books with my learning disability, so I mainly go through the content once and then go for it. If you need to read this one more time, that's cool, but don't keep reading without taking action.

I believe in you probably more than you believe in yourself. You've got the power to do anything you want in this life. The power is right there inside you. Let it out and never look back. If you take some punches to the face, kicks to the gut, and are bulldozed to the ground, know you don't have to stay there waiting for someone to give you a hand up. Get up, dust yourself off, and get back on the horse. Expect bumps, bruises, tears, and sweat to happen. On the other side of your amazing hard work will be exactly what you've desired to achieve. Everyone has different results they want to happen. If you want to live those results, make sure you get crystal clear on your "WHY" for the hard days. As long as your "WHY" is clearly defined, you'll get the hell up and push yourself to win.

REFERENCES

1. "Probate: Definition of Probate by Lexico." Lexico Dictionaries | English. Lexico Dictionaries. Accessed December 21, 2019. https://www.lexico.com/en/definition/probate.

ACKNOWLEDGMENTS

A ROCK-STAR thanks to my attorney, who wrote chapter two, Matthew A. Griffith, Esq. I appreciate you more than you know, buddy. Thanks for being there and helping out with this book.

Big thanks to my brother from another mother, Michael Bredthauer. He's been my best friend who's always been there since 1993. You seriously rock big time, brotha!

Huge shout out to my editor, Hilary Jastram, for helping me wrap up my third book. Without her giving me polite nudges, it may not have crossed the finish line. Thank you!

And many more thank yous go out to those who have had an impact on me over the years and helped to push me on to level up my game:

Jason Palliser, Sal Buscemi, Brecht Palombo, Rod Khleif, Ryan Dossey, Daniil Kleyman, Patrick Riddle, Trevor Mauch, Ken Wade, Cody Sperber, Ross Hamilton, Ed & Bob Diamond, Mark Evans, Josh Cantwell, Jamel Gibbs, Jerry Norton, Stacy Kellams, Chris Prefontaine, Gary Boomershine, Jack Bosch, Zach Braunel, Josh Brown, Cam Dunlap,) Nate Kennedy, Frank Chen, Brian Page, Jeff Coga, Antonio Edwards, Bryan Ellis, Preston Ely, Sean Terry, DC Fawcett, Jim Huntzicker, Frank Kern, Kevin Nations, Joe McCall, Jason Medley, Scott Meyers, Ryan Stewman, DeAnna Rodgers, Mitch Stephen, Zack Childress, Lee Arnold, Adam Adams, Michael Blank, RJ Bates, Julie Houston, Andy Hussong, Nina Klemm, Matt Motil, Kristin

Hayse, Dan Schwartz, Rob Swanson, Brian Trippe, Chris Bruce, Tim Bratz, Brandon & Sam Middleton, Brian Meara, Alex Charfen, Don Costa, Dan Zitofsky, Jeff Watson, David Lecko, Alex Joungblood, Cris Chico, Cory Boatright, Doug Smith, Mike Weiss, Mark Podolsky, Grayson Bouchere (The Professor), Billy Alt, Duane Ortega, Franklin Cruz, Peter Kolat, Peter Vekselman, Jacob Salem, Justin Wilmot, Kathy Fetke, David Corbaley, Eric Medemar, Mark Walters, Mike Hambright, Luke Lee, Marko Rubel, Justin Colby, Kent Clothier, Greg Clement, Lex Levinrad, Wendy Patton, Tamera Aragon, John Cochran, Sam Bell and Chris Rood.

ABOUT THE AUTHOR

Jason Lucchesi founded the real estate investing company, No Flipping Excuses in 2008 after finding quick success in the real estate industry. In 2002, he worked as a loan officer, then joined the nation's #1 lending institution, where he rapidly rose through the ranks to reach the #1 position in the country. After resigning his role, Jason pursued his dream of full-time entrepreneurship through No Flipping Excuses. To date, Jason has partnered on over $285M closed real estate transactions. Jason's expertise includes:

- Working directly with multi-billion-dollar funds
- Distressed Property Expert
- Non-performing and performing notes specialist
- Bulk REO packages
- Wholesaling residential and commercial properties
- Rehabs and new construction
- Multi-Family projects
- Income producing assets
- Tax delinquent properties
- Self-storage facilities

Jason has been married to his wonderful wife, Jamie, since 2007, and they are the proud parents of three children: Brady, Gavin, and Cordelia.

DISCLAIMER

These materials have been prepared by Jason Lucchesi and, in relevant part, Attorney Matthew Griffith. The information and content provided in this book and any summary or excerpt are for informational purposes and are not legal, tax, investment or financial advice, and may or may not reflect the most current legal developments in a particular area. Transmission of the information is not intended to create an attorney-client or other professional relationship and is not intended to constitute legal, tax, investment or financial advice or to substitute for obtaining legal advice from an attorney licensed in your state. Nor is an attorney-client relationship established, merely by reading this book or any part thereof.

CPSIA information can be obtained
at www.ICGtesting.com
Printed in the USA
BVHW091942240220
573162BV00006B/641